DOCUMENTS OF MODERN HISTORY

General Editors:

A. G. Dickens
The Director, Institute of Historical Research, University of London

Alun Davies
Professor of Modern History, University College, Swansea

Already published in this series

The Renaissance Sense of the Past
Peter Burke

Martin Luther
E. G. Rupp and B. Drewery

The Reformation in England to the Accession of Elizabeth I
A. G. Dickens and Dorothy Carr

Erasmus
R. L. De Molen

Education in Tudor and Stuart England
David Cressy

Elizabethan People: State and Society
Joel H. Hurstfield and Alan G. R. Smith

English Colonization of North America
Louis B. Wright and Elaine W. Fowler

Sweden as a Great Power 1611–1697
Michael Roberts

The Divided Society: Party Conflict in England 1694–1716
Geoffrey Holmes and W. A. Speck

The Age of Peel
Norman Gash

The Great Powers and the Near East 1774–1923
M. S. Anderson

Government and Society in France 1814–1848
Irene Collins

Victorian Nonconformity
J. H. Y. Briggs and I. Sellers

Bismarck and Europe
W. N. Medlicott and Dorothy Coveney

The Growth of the British Commonwealth 1880–1932
I. M. Cumpston

From Isolation to Containment: American Foreign Policy 1921–1952
Richard D. Challener

The Diplomacy of World Power: The United States 1889–1920
Arthur S. Link and William M. Leary Jr.

THE REFORMATION
IN ENGLAND

TO THE ACCESSION
OF ELIZABETH I

edited by

A. G. Dickens and Dorothy Carr

Edward Arnold

First published 1967 by
Edward Arnold (Publishers) Ltd.
25 Hill Street, London W1X 8LL
Reprinted 1969
Reprinted 1971
Reprinted 1975

ISBN: 0 7131 5270 2

Printed in Great Britain by
Unwin Brothers Limited
The Gresham Press, Old Woking, Surrey, England
A member of the Staples Printing Group

CONTENTS

PREFACE

Apart from a brief epilogue, this volume ends at 1558. A further volume in the series will include the Elizabethan Settlement and the religious history of Elizabeth's reign.

The amount of documentary material on the subject of the English Reformation is immense: our selection has therefore had to be rigorous. The subject itself is hazardous, especially as the intimate nature of inward spiritual conviction must often remain inaccessible to documentation. Nevertheless, we hope to illustrate that during the first half of the sixteenth century, though undoubtedly many people continued to be attached to the old traditional ways, others were strongly questioning some aspects of late medieval religion, and to some of these critics Protestant doctrines were making a direct appeal. At no time, in no reign, were religious changes merely 'acts of state'.

The words marked with an asterisk * are defined in the glossary on pp. 166-7. In the Introduction, for the sake of clarity, asterisks are placed each time a glossary word occurs; in the rest of the book the asterisk appears only against a word's first occurrence in any particular document. For this purpose, the document is held to include its title and editorial note. Square brackets have been used to indicate all matter not in the original text. Spelling and punctuation have been modernised; archaic words are explained when necessary.

Our thanks are due to the Cambridge University Press, to the Early English Text Society and to the Northamptonshire Record Society for permission to print material in **II, 5**, **III, 11** and **V, 1** respectively.

King's College, London   A. G. D.
September, 1967   D. C.

ABBREVIATIONS

Foxe   John Foxe, *Acts and Monuments* (popularly known as *The Book of Martyrs*), 1563, ed. S. R. Cattley and George Townsend, 8 vols., 1837-1841.
Gee and Hardy   H. Gee and W. J. Hardy, *Documents Illustrative of English Church History*, 1896.
Stat. Realm   *The Statutes of the Realm*, Record Commission, 11 vols., 1810-28.
T.C.L.   *Three Chapters of Letters relating to the Suppression of Monasteries*, ed. Thomas Wright. (*Camden Society*, old series, XXVI, 1843.)

INTRODUCTION

The legal and constitutional aspects of the English Reformation are of enormous importance and have received conspicuous attention. On the one hand Crown and Parliament cut the bonds – spiritual, juridical, financial – which linked the English Church to the Papacy. On the other hand, while leaving the national Church a measure of independent spiritual life, they assumed a tighter control over its powers to legislate, to sanction liturgical forms, to define and enforce beliefs.

This familiar story is nevertheless far from representing the whole process of the Reformation in England. Both the causes and the effects of the movement were also religious, intellectual, social and economic. It left few aspects of national life untouched. As Stuart history shows, it helped to bring forth political changes of great and lasting importance.

In 1520 the religion of the English was predominantly Catholic, yet well before 1600 their religion was predominantly Protestant. This extension of Protestantism was not primarily brought about by acts of State. As in the Netherlands and in Scotland, Protestant beliefs advanced at some stages in the teeth of actual opposition from governments. These beliefs began to affect important groups in English society some years before the Reformation Parliament met. At Antwerp William Tyndale produced and dispatched his New Testament (**II, 4, 5, 7**) under the protection of English merchants who were anything but subservient to the authorities at home. The illegal distribution of such Protestant literature was aided by the secret Lollard communities (**II, 1, 6, 10**) which had tenaciously resisted Church and State for well over a century. Again, during the last years of Henry VIII, when the King tried to eradicate Protestantism, it still appears to have been advancing both at court and throughout the country. Later on Queen Mary brought the whole weight of her government to back the most intensive religious persecution in our history, yet its effect proved the very reverse of her intentions (**VIII, 6, 7**). By the same token, Elizabeth failed to halt the growth of Puritanism – or for that matter to root out Catholicism – by elaborate penal legislation. In view of such facts, our selection of documents cannot be based on the assumption that the English Reformation was a mere State-product, one which can be described by simply reprinting Acts of Parliament, royal and episcopal injunctions and other official precepts.

For all that, State-intervention remains a vital element in this complex process: it helped to mould English religion even while being itself moulded by religious influences. Thus our selection of documents must be designed to show the significance of State-intervention and also to display the Reformation as a process happening in Tudor society, as the story of spirited and questioning human beings. The bitterness of sixteenth-century religious controversy may seem abhorrent to modern readers, yet it will become apparent that this approach often sprang from an immense and unselfish concern for the spiritual health of society.

At various times throughout the middle ages English kings had quarrelled with popes and bishops. From 1309 to 1377 the popes had been resident at Avignon, appearing to be heavily influenced by England's enemy France. Between 1378 and 1417 the Great Schism had seen first two, and finally three popes struggling for universal recognition. And though the Council of Constance (1414-18) had ended the Schism, it had failed to achieve a general reform of the Church. The Council of Basle (1431-49) also failed in this respect and there remained a legacy of discontent in the vital matter of reform. There followed the period of the 'Renaissance' popes, when the papacy had recovered a large measure of its old powers, yet was held in low esteem. As we can now perceive, conditions throughout Europe were becoming more favourable to revolutionary change long before Luther's spectacular protests of 1517-21, but even during the early years of Henry VIII few Englishmen can have felt the imminence of such changes. The English Church remained rich and influential. Many of the King's ministers, diplomats and civil servants were clerics. Laymen went on confessing their sins to their parish priests and answering for their moral lapses in the church courts. Heresy affected only a small part of the nation. The bishops, taking no chances, forbade the dissemination and printing of the Scriptures in the vernacular, but the mystical and doctrinal writers were piously studied by many educated men and women, whilst the veneration of the saints bulked large in the popular religion. Though monasteries were no longer being founded, fine parish churches were still in course of construction; religious guilds flourished and social life in town and country centred largely upon the churches.

On the other hand, the effects of expanding educational opportunities were becoming more manifest among laymen; an unmistakable tone of independence and anticlericalism marked many of the gentry, the officialdom, the lawyers, the merchant-class. Long evident in medieval society, anticlericalism was fostered by many features of ecclesiastical life. Countless lawsuits were waged between laymen and clerics over tithes*. Moreover the monasteries, having been given parochial bene-fices (appropriations*), collected the tithes*, appointed low-paid and often ill-educated chaplains, thus amassing handsome profits. This old grievance and the problem of clerical ignorance in general aroused the wrath of both Catholics like Chancellor Melton (I, 1) and Protestants like Sir Francis Bigod (I, 4). No longer satisfied with ignorant priests merely able to say mass and administer the sacraments, all would-be reformers stressed the importance of a well-endowed, well-educated, teaching clergy – how pointedly at the expense of the monks may be seen in Bigod's *Treatise concerning Impropriations**.

Further disputes arose over mortuary dues payable to the clergy by the relatives of deceased persons. In 1511 the London merchant Richard Hunne quarrelled over this matter with local parish priests. Thence-forth he contentiously brought a series of lawsuits against them and after a search of his house had revealed some heretical literature, he was imprisoned by the bishop on a charge of heresy. In December 1514 he was found murdered in his cell at St. Paul's. The capital seethed with indignation against the church authorities and the scandal was still being recalled when the Reformation Parliament met some fifteen years later. The Hunne affair led immediately to disputes between the bishops and the judges in the King's presence. This was a natural sequel, since the common lawyers, spurred on by their professional jealousy of the canon law, had long welcomed any opportunity to abuse the clergy. We print below (I, 2) a virulent outburst by a lawyer who stood also among the early English Protestants. And while Simon Fish was guilty of gross exaggerations, we have also the earlier testimony of Chancellor Melton and others that unlearned, grasping and lecherous clerics were too common. It seems certain that anticlericalism received a further powerful stimulus from the career of Cardinal Wolsey, who as Lord Chancellor and Papal Legate seemed to monopolise all civil and eccle-siastical powers. His personal ostentation and arrogance did much to provoke the attack of the Commons against the Church in 1529-30.

When Parliament met in November 1529, few of its members were consciously influenced by Protestant teachings and none can have had the slightest inkling of the anti-papal legislation they were destined to pass within a few years. Their initial assault upon ecclesiastical abuses (I, 3) seems the culmination of an old story rather than the beginning of a new one. At the same time, it remains clear that Henry VIII never needed to stir up anticlerical sentiment: as Edward Hall here shows, he had sometimes to moderate the ardour of his lay subjects.

Sections I and II throw light on the origins of the religious Reformation. The Lollard heresy stemming from Wycliffe had been driven underground during the early decades of the fifteenth century, but from about 1490 numerous records testify to its liveliness in London, Essex, the Chilterns, East Anglia, west Kent, the upper Thames Valley and some other areas. It appealed mainly to working people, especially to skilled tradesmen such as clothworkers. The Lollards did not anticipate Luther's key-doctrine of Justification by Faith Alone*, but many of their tendencies (biblicist, anti-saint-worship, anti-sacerdotal, anti-sacramental and anti-papal) resembled those of the Protestant Reformers. John Foxe's accounts (II, 1, 10) can now be confirmed and amplified by reference to many diocesan records. During the 1520s many links were forged between the Lollard groups and the new Lutheranism (II, 6, 10): the former, hitherto much hampered by their lack of printing-presses, now bought Lutheran books and helped in the clandestine book-trade. It may here be added that the wide diffusion of books made possible by the spread of printing became a factor of immense importance for the Reformation, both in England and on the Continent.

The first English Lutherans seem to have emerged from the Cambridge 'White Horse' meetings held from about 1520 under the leadership of Robert Barnes. Concerning these discussions we know practically nothing beyond the meagre details (II, 3) preserved by Foxe. Among the influential figures in Cambridge was also Thomas Bilney, an evangelical individualist rather than a disciple of the continental Reformers: his moving account of his spiritual reflections can be read in II, 2. By far the most important of the early Protestants was William Tyndale, who retired abroad in 1524, visited Wittenberg, settled in Antwerp and in 1526 produced his truly epoch-making translation of the New Testament. This work, backed by the polemical treatises of Tyndale and his collaborators, proved a most weighty factor in the early expansion of Protestantism in England (**II, 4, 5** and **VI, 2**). Their impact owed much to inadequate policing by the agents of the bishops and to the ingenuity (**II, 7**) of Protestant merchants and book-sellers. The London traders and their colleagues stationed in Antwerp formed the backbone of this organisation. Others brought back to lesser towns first-hand accounts of Protestantism in north Germany and the Netherlands (**II, 8**), though they did not necessarily understand all they saw. Meanwhile amongst intellectuals the movement spread from Cambridge to Oxford, notably to Wolsey's new Cardinal College. The melodramatic adventures in Oxford of the important agent Thomas Garret may be followed in **II, 9**.

Doctrinally speaking, Protestantism involved far more than an attack upon saint-worship, pilgrimages, indulgences, the doctrine of purga-tory★ and the shortcomings of the priesthood. It demanded the educa-tion of both clergy and laity in the vernacular Scriptures; it sought to determine problems of morality, church life and public worship by reference to Scriptural authority, as distinct from practices and tradi-tions which had arisen since Apostolic times. It tended to place preach-ing before the sacraments and to regard transubstantiation★ as a mere three-centuries-old invention by the Aristotelian schoolmen. Yet its own attempts at a more authentic doctrine of the mass varied from the 'real presence' as defined by Luther to the Zwinglian interpretation which pronounced the rite to be symbolic. Even at this early date, some Englishmen like John Frith (**II, 11**) leaned strongly toward the latter. Under Henry VIII as under Mary, nearly all the Protestant martyrs were to die for denying transubstantiation★. Nevertheless, the most basic Protestant doctrine concerned Justification, the manner in which man enters into a saving relationship with God. On this issue Luther's solifidian★ interpretation of St. Paul found general support from Zwingli, Calvin and most other leading Protestant churchmen. Con-trary to the teaching generally held, Luther urged that men are justified not by any merits of their own, in the form of religious observances and other good works. Justification comes solely from the merits of Christ, which are imputed (i.e. reckoned) to our credit. They are imputed not by any gradual process of cleansing, but suddenly as a whole, and are appropriated by faith. This faith is given by God to predestined recipients, and while man possesses free will in regard to the ordinary affairs of life, on the plane of salvation he remains alto-gether incapable of making any contribution from his own feeble re-sources. While good works are the inevitable result of Justification, they can never be its cause. The practical implications of this highly Christocentric and predestinarian teaching are explained in Tyndale's *Prologue to Romans* (**II, 5**), which is freely translated from Luther's original.

As observed, the Henrician Reformation of the 1530s must be sharply distinguished from the advent into England of Protestant doctrines: the special characteristics which mark the doctrinal and disciplinary statements of the late 1530s (**IV**) will be discussed later. Though Henry's chief minister (1532-40) Thomas Cromwell and his new archbishop Thomas Cranmer were strongly attracted toward Lutheranism, Henry himself retained conservative views on all points of doctrine apart from the Papal Supremacy. So did the great majority of his bishops and nobles, led by Bishop Gardiner and the Duke of Norfolk. To begin with, Henry's legislation sprang mainly from the royal divorce suit, which, if it did not 'cause' the English Reformation, certainly affected its timing and its character. The day-to-day details of the suit have little relevance to our subject, and cannot here be illustrated by brief documentation. No one who understands the delicate balance of the Tudor State can doubt that Henry and the realm desperately needed a male heir and an indisputable succession. Throughout the Henrician documents there occurs a constant emphasis on 'unity and concord', the overwhelming practical consideration of the time. Henry's failure at Rome resulted from the hard fact that Queen Katherine's nephew the Emperor Charles V gained military control over Rome from about the time that Henry started his proceedings. This factor decided the issue, even though Henry's legal case was fairly strong, the precedents for royal divorces impressive, the intentions of Pope Clement VII conciliatory. By 1529-30 Wolsey's failure to manipulate the Curia had become evident: on his consequent dismissal his successor Norfolk was soon telling the Imperial ambassador that papal jurisdiction was in any case invalid in England.

The Pardon of the Clergy, the Supplication of the Commons, the Submission of the Clergy (**III, 1-3**) gave the King more control over the national Church without securing the divorce. The Submission of the Clergy to the King did not mean the abolition of ecclesiastical courts, which in fact continued far beyond the sixteenth century to deal with cases arising from wills or matrimonial matters, and with charges of immorality. In 1532 had come the rise to power of Wolsey's former business agent Thomas Cromwell, who drafted the long sequence of Acts restricting and then abolishing papal authority, replacing it by a Royal Supremacy, transferring papal taxation to the Crown, and markedly increasing the Crown's financial demands on the Church (**III, 4-9**). Having started with the special problem of the divorce, Cromwell ended by reshaping the relations of Church, State and society. These Acts were truly revolutionary, yet they were not entirely independent of medieval precedents and precepts. In attacking clerical privilege, the Crown used the *Praemunire** legislation of the fourteenth century, which had been loosely drafted and could be strained to threaten any Englishman introducing papal bulls or 'foreign' jurisdiction into the realm. Again, the erastian* theories elaborated early in that same century by Marsiglio of Padua were now expressed forcibly by the 'Henrician Catholic' Stephen Gardiner to justify the Royal Supremacy (**III, 10**), while Thomas Cromwell personally financed the publication in English of Marsiglio's *Defensor Pacis*. It would be difficult to write a better thumbnail sketch of Marsiglio's position than the one found in the famous preamble to the Act in Restraint of Appeals (**III, 5**), or a sharper repudiation of that position than the speech by Sir Thomas More at his trial (**III, 11**).

Alongside this legislation the King ruled the national Church through Proclamations and Injunctions, while doctrinal formularies were drawn up at his command. It is interesting to find that whereas the King's supreme authority over the English Church had been most clearly affirmed, the subsequent doctrinal and disciplinary statements of the years 1536-8 (**IV, 1-5**) were much less decisive and at no time markedly dogmatic. Rather are they tentative and adiaphorist*, moving towards an independent position which foreshadows that of the fully-developed Anglican Church. Stress is laid less on formal outward observance than on inward piety and practice of the Christian ethic, on the obedience and honour due to God's word, which should be authoritatively interpreted by a respected pastorate to a responsible laity. This whole approach owed a good deal to the influence of Erasmus (*c.* 1466-1536), whose edition of the Greek New Testament, with a new translation into Latin, had made a great appeal in England (**II, 2, 9**).

Arising out of this approach there had developed a very critical attitude towards practices alleged to be superstitious. This became a marked feature of the whole English Reformation, and was to be at its most vigorous during the reign of Edward VI (**VII, 3**). It is first seen officially in the years 1536-8, notably in the First and Second Royal Injunctions (**IV, 3, 4**). In these comprehensive Injunctions a constructive effort was made to promote a spiritual welfare which would necessarily engender social welfare within the 'common weal'. They were issued by Cromwell in his capacity as Henry's vicegerent, an office which allowed his commands to override those of the bishops. The Injunctions run parallel with the political and social writings of Cromwell's chief publicist Thomas Starkey. Their interest is far more than purely ecclesiastical and they show a deep awareness of the contemporary links between religion, education and social conduct.

An equally characteristic example of Cromwellian activity is the *Valor Ecclesiasticus* (**V, 1**), a revised assessment of all ecclesiastical incomes, enabling the Crown to collect in full the taxation recently assigned by Parliament (**III, 9**). The *Valor* also had its uses in connection with the impending dissolution of religious houses, the stages and methods of which are explained and illustrated in **V, 2, 3, 5, 6**. The earnest and reasoned plea for the retention of the monasteries made by Robert Aske, leader of the Pilgrimage of Grace in 1536, may be read in **V, 4**.

In 1535 a number of the London Carthusians had heroically suffered death rather than admit the King's Supremacy, yet the great bulk of monks and nuns (who numbered about 9,300) took their pensions and accepted the new world. Though English monasticism had with a few exceptions become lifeless and uninspired, its sudden and total abolition marked a long step towards the remodelling of the nation's religious and social life. Cromwell, who in earlier life had dissolved many small religious houses on behalf of his master Wolsey, now envisaged this general dissolution in order to create a vast and permanent landed endowment for the Crown. In the event, between his fall in 1540 and Henry's death in 1547 by far the greater part of the monastic lands were sold off to pay for the wars against France and Scotland. This huge transfer is no longer thought to have proved catastrophic for the tenants and workers on the monastic estates. In general, the monasteries themselves had not been easy-going landlords. As for the new lay owners, they were likewise realists, yet the great majority were members of the established gentry families whose desire for prestige in the county could hardly be reconciled with rack-renting or other violent innovations. In addition, the general rise in food-prices greatly favoured the tenant-farmers and yeomen who paid rent to the gentry. It is also certain that men bought monastic lands irrespective of their own religious leanings. In Mary's reign the Imperial ambassador rightly informed his master 'that the Catholics hold more church property than do the heretics'.

In 1539-40 the King, irritated both by attacks on transubstantiation* and by the failure of the Cleves marriage into which Cromwell had led him, allowed the conservatives Norfolk and Gardiner to persuade him into a policy of reaction. Norfolk introduced the Six Articles Act with its ferocious penalties (**VI, 1**). Cromwell was attainted for heresy and treason; then over the succeeding years a few Protestants were burned, of whom Anne Askew (see **VI, 5**) became the most famous. While in 1537 the semi-official *Bishops' Book* (**IV, 5**) had to some extent reflected Protestant influences, it was now replaced in 1543 by the much more Catholic *King's Book* (**VI, 3**). Nevertheless, Protestant literature continued to circulate, and an Act of 1543 (see **VI, 3**) to limit Bible-reading to the upper classes appears to have proved ineffectual. The religious phraseology of wills indicates a steady advance of Protestant opinions, while at court magnates like Edward Seymour Earl of Hertford (later Protector Somerset) cautiously favoured them. The King himself protected Cranmer against charges of heresy and sanctioned the use of his English Litany (1544) in the churches. Cranmer even composed an English communion-service, though he was not encouraged to publish it in Henry's lifetime. In May 1545 an English Primer (a book of Prayers) was authorised by royal proclamation. Meanwhile the young Prince Edward was being instructed by Dr. Richard Cox and Sir John Cheke, men whose Protestant sympathies must have been widely known. Certainly Henry's policy of reaction was fitfully applied and he was possibly beginning to see that his brand of orthodoxy might not after all prove permanent. In his famous speech made to Parliament in December 1545 (**VI, 4**) he made a strong plea for charity and concord. When he died in January 1547 it so happened that Norfolk was in prison for concealing the treason of his son Surrey, while even Bishop Gardiner had been excluded by the irascible royal invalid from the proposed Council of Regency.

This situation proved wholly favourable to the assumption of near-regal powers by Somerset. Though a sincere Protestant and on friendly terms with Calvin, the Protector was also an erastian* who sent royal commissioners to inspect the Church, issued Injunctions closely based on those of Thomas Cromwell, appointed bishops by letters patent (see **VII, 1**) and passed an Act assigning to the Crown the lands of chantries* and many other foundations (**VII, 3 4**). This last measure severely affected parish life, yet many of these institutions were already moribund, while the chantry schools, together with the more necessary parochial chapels and almshouses, were refounded. On the other hand, Somerset pursued a far more liberal policy than that of Henry, removing laws which prohibited the marriage of priests (**VII, 6**) and repealing the Six Articles Act (**VI, 1**), the old statute *de Haeretico Comburendo*, the oppressive Henrician treason-laws and all restrictions on printing, reading or teaching the Scriptures. Despite Somerset's Act against Revilers (**VII, 1**) the years 1548-9 saw many bitter attacks on the Catholic doctrines of the mass, while the local disputes are well illustrated by Thomas Hancock's narrative (**VII, 2**). It is interesting to find Hancock speaking here of the people of Poole as 'the first that in that part of England were called Protestants'. Throughout Edward's reign, doctrinal controversy continued to centre upon the sacrament of the altar. Both the moderate and the more radical Reformers wanted communion for the laity in both bread and wine, and following a proposal by Convocation in November 1547 this received legislative sanction in the first Parliament of the reign (**VII, 1**). The Reformers also agreed in denying that each mass was a re-enactment of Christ's sacrifice on the Cross, and in maintaining that the Crucifixion was in itself 'sufficient sacrifice, oblation and satisfaction for the sins of the whole world' – a logical development from the doctrine of Justification by Faith Alone*. While denouncing transubstantiation*, the Reformers continued to differ among themselves concerning the nature of the divine presence in the eucharist. Cranmer's own beliefs on this matter changed and developed over the years. The Reformers also differed over 'externals': as to which vestments should be worn, whether tables should replace altars, and if so where in the chancel the table should stand. These issues were progressively dealt with in the Edwardian Prayer Books and Acts of Uniformity (**VII, 5, 7**).

In March 1548 Cranmer's *Order of Communion* provided English prayers to be inserted in the Latin mass in order that the provisions of the Act for Receiving in Both Kinds (**VII, 1**) could be implemented. Shortly afterwards mass, matins and evensong, all in English, were allowed in St. Paul's and some other London churches. In September the Archbishop was discussing his first English Prayer Book with a group of divines. By January 1549 it had been approved by both Houses of Parliament and having received the royal sanction it came into operation on Whitsunday 9 June, enforced by an Act of Uniformity with graduated penalties (**VII, 5**). In this Prayer Book Cranmer for the first time comprehended all the rites of the national Church within one volume. With great success he fused together a number of liturgies both Catholic and Lutheran. The order of the Latin mass and the medieval vestments he largely retained, and though he intended to remove all notions of transubstantiation* and sacrifice, even Bishop Gardiner (now in prison) embarrassingly declared his readiness to use this conservative and sometimes ambiguous Book. So far as the Revolts in the summer of 1549 are concerned, while the followers of Kett in Norfolk accepted the Book, the majority of rebels in the more conservative areas of Devon and Cornwall decisively rejected it.

In the subsequent autumn Somerset was overthrown by the opportunist John Dudley Earl of Warwick, later made Duke of Northumberland. Dudley soon began to favour the advanced Protestants, John Hooper and John Knox, who came increasingly under the influence of the Swiss Reformers. Meanwhile, supported by Nicholas Ridley Bishop of London and counselled by Martin Bucer the distinguished exile from Strassburg, the Archbishop himself started remodelling his Prayer Book along distinctly more Protestant lines. Nevertheless there remain doubts regarding the extent of his personal responsibility for the ensuing revisions. In May 1550 Ridley substituted tables for altars in his diocese and the Privy Council ordered the other bishops to do likewise. In April 1552 a further Act of Uniformity (**VII, 7**) enforced the use of the revised Prayer Book as from 1 November. Whatever the influence of Bucer and the many other learned refugees now in England, this Second Book did not seek to reproduce Zwinglian or Calvinist forms of service. Its key-note is the text, 'Do this in remembrance of me.' The central structure of the mass is altered to avoid a solemn, sacrificial approach, while the priest's words of administration stress the aspects of commemoration and thanksgiving. The table is to be placed in an east-west position, not altar-wise, the priest standing on the north side. Medieval vestments are forbidden and the use of the surplice is enjoined. Even now men like Hooper and Knox did not feel satisfied. Seeing that the Book directed communicants to kneel, these enthusiasts urged the Council to make Cranmer rescind this order. Following the Archbishop's refusal, the Council on its own authority added to the Book the so-called Black Rubric, denying that kneeling implied any adoration of the bread and wine, or the presence therein of Christ's natural body.

Alongside this Second Prayer Book Cranmer drew up a much-needed scheme to reform the canon law, but he failed to secure its adoption. More important, he took the lead in compiling the Forty-two Articles of Religion, which received the royal assent on 12 June 1553, less than a month before the young King's death. The Articles formed a decisively Protestant interpretation of the Faith; they accepted Calvinist predestinarian teaching and condemned the sacrificial concept of the mass, together with the doctrine of purgatory★ and the adoration of saints and images. Some articles are also directed against the Anabaptists★, who had begun to come over from the Netherlands during the thirties, had suffered heavy persecution, but were now making some English converts. The Forty-two Articles were to be revised by the Elizabethans in 1563 and to become the famous Thirty-nine, still the official formulary of the Church of England. A strong denunciation of the Second Prayer Book and of the whole Edwardian Reformation is made in Robert Parkyn's narrative, extracts from which are given in **VII, 8**.

These last years of Edward VI saw the continuance of the Reformation under Northumberland's near-bankrupt government, which resorted even to the confiscation of surplus plate from the parish churches. While the reputation of Protestantism was undoubtedly tarnished through its association with desperate politicians, elements of religious and social idealism did not vanish from its thinking. A Protestant-humanist group usually known as the 'Commonwealth Men' was inspired by Bishop Latimer and had among its leaders the enclosures commissioner John Hales and one of the secretaries of state, Sir Thomas Smith. These men denounced covetous landlords and called for a greater degree of social justice. Likewise relevant to an assessment of the Edwardian Reformation are those several writers (including William Turner, Dean of Wells) who stressed the evils of juridical persecution and believed that spiritual failings – even those of the Anabaptists★ – should be fought not by fire and the stake but by spiritual weapons, by the teaching of a clergy armed 'with the sword of God's word'.

On the death of Edward VI, Northumberland's plot to secure the succession for his daughter-in-law Lady Jane Grey speedily collapsed. Most Englishmen, whatever their religious leanings, believed it necessary to ensure the legitimate succession in the person of the Princess Mary; even Protestants were in general willing to run the risks suggested by her courageous and ardent practice of the Catholic religion. Once she had ascended the throne, Mary had to impose her religious settlement by royal authority upon a largely sluggish people: she was then left with the much harder task of promoting a Catholic religious revival. The call by her exiled cousin Cardinal Pole for an immediate submission to the Papacy was sternly countered by her other cousin the Emperor Charles, who dreaded lest the proposed marriage between Mary and his son Philip should be endangered by precipitate

Catholic zeal and consequent disorder in England. The Marian reaction passed through two distinct phases. The Queen's first Parliament abrogated Edward's Protestant Statutes and thus restored the legal situation obtaining in the last year of Henry VIII (**VIII, 1**). In March 1554 Mary sent her Injunctions to the bishops (**VIII, 2**). Later in the same year her third Parliament uneasily agreed to revive the heresy laws, to repeal Henry VIII's anti-papal legislation and to restore the situation of 1529 (**VIII, 3, 4**). This second stage was gradually rendered possible in 1554 by the failure of Sir Thomas Wyatt's anti-Spanish rising, by the apparent public acceptance of the Queen's marriage and by Pope Julius III, who in effect authorised Pole to leave the laity in possession of the former church lands.

For the governing and landed classes this last issue had become paramount, and even the convinced Catholics had not the slightest intention of restoring to the Church the lands for which they had paid the Crown good money. Once Mary's Second Statute of Repeal (**VIII, 4**) confirmed their ownership, many laymen were quite prepared to let Pole (who returned as Papal Legate to absolve the realm) and the clerical party stage a religious persecution. After all these changes, the prevalent mood of the nation had tended to become secular and disillusioned. The ardent Protestants and the ardent Catholics seem to have formed small minorities of the population. With few exceptions the justices of the peace proved markedly unenthusiastic when it came to the arrests and the burnings. In the south-east, where by far the greater number of the martyrs suffered, many instances of popular sympathy are recorded. These may well have sprung less from Protestant zeal or from mere humanitarianism than from a lack of positive Catholic fervour, a lack of horror against heresy, and a growing hatred of Spain.

The Marian reaction betrays an intellectual and religious sterility uncharacteristic of the Catholic Reformation then enlivening so many parts of Europe. The Queen was able to restore only six religious houses, having a mere hundred monks between them. Pole could have modernised his weapons by bringing members of the newly-founded Society of Jesus to work in England but he failed to do so. By contrast, the martyrdoms of distinguished Protestant divines like Latimer, Ridley, John Bradford and Rowland Taylor did much to re-inspire the Protestants, who at least in London became highly organised and ever more numerous (**VIII, 6, 7**). Despite some waverings under pressure during his long period of imprisonment, Cranmer himself contrived to make a deep impression by his last superb gesture at the stake. Moreover some 800 English emigrants, most of them able, educated and well-connected people, formed congregations and published propaganda at Frankfurt, Zürich, Strassburg, Geneva and other continental cities. Amid the quarrels at Frankfurt between the Calvinists headed by John Knox and those who strove to retain the Second Edwardian Prayer Book (**VIII, 5**), even the latter tended to imbibe Calvinist as opposed to Lutheran ideas. They were destined not only to dominate the Elizabethan Settlement of 1559 but also to sow the seeds of Puritanism within the Elizabethan Church. Their chance came much sooner than any can have supposed when leaving England. Mary's unpopularity continued to grow. Added to the effects of a bitter quarrel between the anti-Spanish Pope Paul IV and the unfortunate Cardinal Pole, an exceptional number of Mary's bishops died during the year 1558. Hence when Mary and Pole died within a few hours of each other in November 1558 the Catholic cause stood in utter disarray. Tired of religious vicissitudes, of fanaticism and of Spanish influence, all save the few ardent Marians welcomed the accession of the Princess Elizabeth, whose background, upbringing and personal repute all promised a settlement based solely upon English interests.

I

CRITICISM OF THE CLERGY

1 Chancellor Melton's Exhortation

William Melton, D.D., was Master of Michaelhouse, Cambridge, and tutor to the future Bishop John Fisher. In 1496 he became Chancellor of York Minster, which office he held until his death in 1528. Like his friend Dean Colet and many medieval predecessors, he felt deeply the need to raise the intellectual and moral standards of the parish clergy. The subsequent extract is translated from a long Latin sermon addressed to ordinands in the diocese of York, and published about 1510.

For it is from this stupidity and from this darkness of ignorance that there arises that great and deplorable evil throughout the whole Church of God, that everywhere throughout town and countryside there exists a crop of oafish and boorish priests, some of whom are engaged on ignoble and servile tasks, while others abandon themselves to tavern-haunting, swilling and drunkenness. Some cannot get along without their wenches; others pursue their amusement in dice and gambling and other such trifling all day long. There are some who waste their time in hunting and hawking, and so spend a life which is utterly and wholly slothful and irreligious even to advanced old age. This is inevitable, for since they are all completely ignorant of good literature, how can they obtain improvement or enjoyment in reading and study? Nay rather, they throw aside their books in contempt and everywhere they return to the wretched and unlovely life I have mentioned, and seek to satisfy their sloth and idleness in trifles of this sort. . . .

We must avoid and keep far from ourselves that grasping, deadly plague of avarice for which practically every priest is accused and held in disrepute before the people, when it is said that we are greedy for rich promotions, or harsh and grasping in retaining or amassing money, and spend but little or nothing on works of piety. For shame! How notorious are we for cunning in making contracts! How absorbed we are in careful purchases or profitable sales! These men take up the fields, the richest pastures, so that their herds of cattle and flocks of sheep may enjoy the finest grazing, but they take neither thought nor care for the tending of their own souls. Because of such people is the honour of the holy priesthood profaned and defiled. Under Christ's teaching, let us beware lest our hearts be oppressed by tipsiness and drunkenness, and let us therefore avoid the guzzling of boon companions and tavern-company. For there is nothing more disgraceful than a tipsy, drunken cleric. Finally, we must be most vigilant that our whole life should not appear idle and slothful, full of sluggishness and vanity.

Sermo exhortatorius cancelarii Ebor[*acensis*]
(W. de Worde, *c.* 1510), sig. A iii

2   Simon Fish on Clerical Vices

Simon Fish entered Gray's Inn about 1525, and having incurred Wolsey's displeasure fled to Holland, where he wrote *A Supplication for the Beggars*, probably published in 1529. He also translated from the Dutch the Protestant tract *The Sum of Scripture* (Antwerp, 1529, and later going through five English editions, 1535-50). Fish died in 1531 soon after his return, his widow marrying the Protestant martyr James Bainham. Despite its misrepresentations, the *Supplication* echoed the suspicions and prejudices of many lay readers. It is written in the form of a plea to Henry VIII from the poor, sick and needy.

These are not the [shep]herds but the ravenous wolves going in [shep]herds' clothing, devouring the flock: the bishops, abbots, priors, deacons, archdeacons, suffragans, priests, monks, canons, friars, pardoners and summoners. And who is able to number this idle, ravenous sort, which (setting all labour aside) have begged so importunately that they have gotten into their hands more than the third part of all your realm. The goodliest lordships, manors, lands and territories are theirs. Besides this they have the tenth part of all the corn, meadow, pasture, grass, wool, colts, calves, lambs, pigs, geese and chickens. Over and besides, the tenth part of every servant's wages, the tenth part of the wool, milk, honey, wax, cheese and butter. Yea, and they look so narrowly upon their profits that the poor wives must be countable to them of every tenth egg, or else she . . . shall be taken as an heretic. . . .

What money pull they in by probates of testaments, privy tithes*, and

by men's offerings to their pilgrimages and at their first masses? Every
man and child that is buried must pay somewhat for masses and *diriges*
to be sung for him, or else they will accuse the dead's friends and
executors of heresy. . . . What a multitude of money gather the pardoners in a year? How much money get the summoners by extortion
in a year, by citing people to the commissary's court and afterward
releasing the appearance for money? Finally, the infinite number of
begging friars; what get they in a year? . . .

And what do all this greedy sort of sturdy, idle, holy thieves, with
these yearly exactions that they take of the people? Truly nothing, but
exempt themselves from the obedience of your Grace! Nothing, but
translate all rule, power, lordship, authority, obedience and dignity
from your Grace unto them! Nothing, but that all your subjects should
fall into disobedience and rebellion against your Grace, and be under
them; as they did unto your noble predecessor King John. . . . For
which matter your most noble realm wrongfully (alas for shame!) hath
stood tributary, not unto any kind of temporal prince, but unto a
cruel, devilish blood-supper, drunken in the blood of the saints and
martyrs of Christ ever since. . . .

Yea, and what do they more? Truly, nothing but apply themselves, by
all the sleights they may, to have to do with every man's wife, every
man's daughter, and every man's maid, that cuckoldry and bawdry
should reign over all among your subjects, that no man should know
his own child; that their bastards might inherit the possessions of every
man, to put the right-begotten children clear beside their inheritance,
in subversion of all estates and godly order. . . . These be they that have
made a hundred thousand idle, [dissolute women] in your realm, who
would have gotten their living honestly, in the sweat of their faces, had
not their [the clergy's] superfluous riches [allured] them to unclean lust
and idleness. . . .

So captive are your laws unto them, that no man that they list to
excommunicate may be admitted to sue any action in any of your
courts. If any man in your sessions dare be so hardy to indict a priest
of any such crime, he hath, ere the year go out, such a yoke of heresy
laid on his neck, that it maketh him wish that he had not done it. Had
not Richard Hunne commenced an action of *Praemunire**★** against a
priest, he had been yet alive, and no heretic at all, but an honest man.
Did not divers of your noble progenitors, seeing their crown and
dignity run into ruin . . . make divers statutes for the reformation

thereof, among which the Statute of Mortmain was one, to the intent that after that time they should have no more given unto them? But what availed it? Have they not gotten into their hands more lands since, than any duke in England hath, the Statute notwithstanding? ... Oh, how all the substance of your realm (your sword, power, crown, dignity and obedience of your people) runneth headlong into the insatiable whirlpool of these greedy gulfs, to be swallowed and devoured! ...

But there be many men of great literature and judgment, that for the love they have unto the truth and unto the commonwealth, have not feared to put themselves into the greatest infamy that may be ... yea, in peril of death, to declare their opinion in this matter: which is that there is no purgatory*, but that it is a thing invented by the covetousness of the spiritualty, only to translate all kingdoms from other princes unto them, and that there is not one word spoken of it in all holy Scripture. They say also that if there were a purgatory, and also if the Pope with his pardons may for money deliver one soul thence, he may deliver him as well without money: if he may deliver one, he may deliver a thousand: if he may deliver a thousand, he may deliver them all; and so destroy purgatory: and then he is a cruel tyrant, without all charity, if he keep them there in prison and in pain, till men will give him money.... Wherefore it is manifest it cannot be of Christ, for he gave more to the temporal kingdom; he himself paid tribute to Caesar; he took nothing from him, but taught that the high powers should be always obeyed.... This is the great scab why they will not let the New Testament go abroad in your mother tongue, lest men should espy that they by their cloaked hypocrisy do translate thus fast your kingdom into their hands; that they are not obedient unto your high power; that they are cruel, unclean, unmerciful and hypocrites; that they seek not the honour of Christ, but their own; that remission of sins is not given by the Pope's pardon, but by Christ, for the sure faith and trust that we have in him....

But what remedy to relieve us, your poor, sick, lame and sore beadsmen? To make hospitals for the relief of the poor people? Nay, truly. The more the worse, for ever the fat of the whole foundation hangeth on the priests' beards. Divers of your noble predecessors, kings of this realm, have given lands to monasteries, to give a certain sum of money yearly to the poor people, whereof ... they give never one penny.... Wherefore if your Grace will build a sure hospital that never shall fail to relieve us all your poor beadsmen, so take from them all these things. Set these sturdy loobies abroad in the world, to get them wives of their own, to get their living with their labour in the sweat of their faces, according to the commandment of God, *Genesis* iii, to give other idle people, by their example, occasion to go to labour.

Tie these holy idle thieves to the carts, to be whipped naked about every market town till they will fall to labour, that they by their importunate begging take not away the alms that the good Christian people would give unto us, sore, impotent, miserable people, your beadsmen. Then shall as well the number of our aforesaid monstrous sort, as of the [profligate men and women], thieves and idle people, decrease; then shall these great yearly exactions cease; then shall not your sword, power, crown, dignity, and obedience of your people be translated from you; then shall you have full obedience of your people; then shall the idle people be set to work; then shall matrimony be much better kept: then shall the generation of your people be increased; then shall your commons increase in riches; then shall the gospel be preached; then shall none beg our alms from us; then shall we have enough, and more than shall suffice us; which shall be the best hospital that ever was founded for us; then shall we daily pray to God for your most noble estate long to endure.

Simon Fish, *A Supplicacyon for the Beggers* (1529)
(reprinted *Early English Text Society*, ed. F. J.
Furnivall, extra series, xiii, 1871), pp. 1-15

3 Opening Scenes of the Reformation Parliament

Edward Hall, the contemporary chronicler who consistently makes a hero of the King and villains of the clergy, describes here the anticlerical outbursts which marked the opening stages of the Reformation Parliament. The latter met on 4 November 1529, a few days after proceedings had been initiated in the King's Bench against Wolsey. The events here recorded were followed by three Statutes (21 Hen. VIII, cap. 5, 6, 13) limiting fees for the probate of wills, defining mortuary dues and limiting pluralism* and non-residence*, together with trading and farming by the clergy.

When the Commons were assembled in the nether House they began to common of their griefs wherewith the spiritualty had beforetime grievously oppressed them, both contrary to the law of the realm, and contrary to all right, and in especial they were sore moved with six great causes.

The first for the excess fines, which the Ordinaries* took for probate of testaments, insomuch that Sir Henry Guildford, Knight of the Garter and Comptroller of the King's house, declared in the open Parliament on his fidelity that he and others, being executors to Sir William Compton, Knight, paid for the probate of his will to the Cardinal and the Archbishop of Canterbury a thousand mark sterling [£666]: after this declaration were showed so many extortions done by Ordinaries for probates of wills that it were too much to rehearse.

The second cause was the great polling and extreme exaction, which the spiritual men used in taking of corpse presents or mortuaries, for the children of the defunct should all die for hunger and go abegging rather than they would of charity give to them the silly [simple, poor] cow which the dead man owed, if he had but only one, such was the charity then.

The third cause was, that priests being surveyors, stewards and officers to bishops, abbots and other spiritual heads, had and occupied farms, granges and grazing in every country [district], so that the poor husbandmen could have nothing but of them, and yet for that they should pay dearly. The fourth cause was that abbots, priors and spiritual men kept tan-houses, and bought and sold wool, cloth and all manner of merchandise as other temporal merchants did. The fifth cause, was because the spiritual persons promoted to great benefices and having their living of their flock, were lying in the court in the lords' houses, and took all of the parishioners, and nothing spent on them at all, so that for lack of residence both the poor of the parish lacked refreshing, and universally all the parishioners lacked preaching and true instruction of God's word, to the great peril of their souls.

The sixth cause was to see one priest being little learned to have ten or twelve benefices and to be resident on none, and to know many well-learned scholars in the university, which were able to preach and teach, to have neither benefice nor exhibition.

These things before this time might in nowise be touched nor yet talked of by no man except he would be made a heretic, or lose all that he had, for the bishops were Chancellors, and had all the rule about the King, so that no man durst once presume to attempt anything contrary to their profit, or commodity. But now when God had illumined the eyes of the King, and that their subtle doings was once espied, then men began charitably to desire a reformation, and so at this Parliament men began to show their grudges.

Whereupon the burgesses of the Parliament appointed such as were learned in the law, being of the Common House, to draw one bill of the probates of testaments, another for mortuaries, and the third for non-residence, pluralities, and taking of farms by spiritual men. The learned men took much pain, and first set forth the bill of mortuaries, which passed the Common House and was sent up to the Lords. To this bill the spiritual Lords made a fair face, saying that surely priests and curates took more than they should, and therefore it were well done to take some reasonable order; thus they spake because it touched them little.

But within two days after was sent up the bill concerning probates of testaments, at the which the Archbishop of Canterbury [William Warham, d. 1532] in especial and all other bishops in general both frowned and grunted, for that touched their profit; insomuch as Doctor John Fisher, Bishop of Rochester, said openly in the Parliament chamber these words: 'My lords, you see daily what bills come hither from the Common House and all is to the destruction of the Church. For God's sake see what a realm the Kingdom of Bohemia was, and when the Church went down, then fell the glory of the Kingdom. Now with the Commons is nothing but down with the Church, and all this me seemeth is for lack of faith only.'

When these words were reported to the Commons of the nether house, that the Bishop should say that all their doings were for lack of faith, they took the matter grievously, for they imagined that the Bishop esteemed them as heretics, and so by his slanderous words would have persuaded the temporal Lords to have restrained their consent from the said two bills, which they before had passed, as you have heard before.

Wherefore the Commons after long debate determined to send the Speaker of the Parliament to the King's Highness with a grievous complaint against the Bishop of Rochester, and so on a day when the King was at leisure Thomas Audley the Speaker for the Commons and thirty of the chief of the Common House came to the King's presence ... and there very eloquently declared what a dishonour to the King and the realm it was to say that they which were elected for the wisest men of all the shires, cities and boroughs within the realm of England should be declared in so noble and open presence to lack faith, which was equivalent to say that they were infidels and no Christians, as ill as Turks or Saracens, so that what pain or study soever they took for the commonwealth, or what acts or laws soever they made or stablished, should be taken as laws made by paynims and heathen people, and not worthy to be kept by Christian men. Wherefore he most humbly besought the King's Highness to call the said Bishop before him, and to cause him to speak more discreetly of such a number as was in the Common House.

The King was not well contented with the saying of the Bishop, yet he gently answered the Speaker that he would send for the Bishop, and send them word what answer he made, and so they departed again. After this the King sent for the Archbishop of Canterbury and six other bishops, and for the Bishop of Rochester also, and there declared to him the grudge of the Commons, to the which the Bishop answered that he meant the doings of the Bohemians was for lack of faith, and not the doings of them that were in the Common House; which saying was confirmed by the bishops being present, which had him in great reputation; and so by that only saying the King accepted his excuse and therefore sent word to the Commons by Sir William Fitzwilliam, Knight, Treasurer of his Household, which blind excuse pleased the Commons nothing at all.

Edward Hall, Henry VIII (1548), ed. C.Whibley (1904), ii.165-8

4   Sir Francis Bigod on Impropriations* and Preachers

Sir Francis Bigod (1507-37), heir to broad lands in Yorkshire, was a ward of Wolsey and studied at Oxford, where he probably imbibed Protestant opinions. In later years Thomas Garret (see **II, 9**) was his chaplain. Active in the North as an agent of Thomas Cromwell, Bigod at last fell foul of the government and was executed for attempting to revive the reactionary Pilgrimage of Grace, 1536-7 (see **V, 4**). This movement he joined, however, without altering his own Protestant views. Bigod's attack on monastic impropriations (*c.* 1535) has been too little noticed; his demand for a well-endowed teaching clergy is constructive and foreshadows that of the Elizabethan Puritans.

But now considering, most benign Sovereign Lord, how much all your subjects be imperpetually bound to laud, praise and glorify Almighty God, to send unto us so Christian a King to have rule and governance over us your subjects, by whose great and inestimable diligent labour, charge, study and pain, we be delivered from the hard, sharp and ten thousand times more than judicial captivity of that Babylonical man of Rome, to the sweet and soft service, yea, rather liberty of the gospel, I can for my part no less do, than to present to your Grace something thereby to declare how gladly I would give thanks to your Highness for such profit as I among others have received by this said benefit in our deliverance, which act is of itself so highly to the great peace, unity and wealth of this most noble Empire of England. . . .

To recite in one volume, good Christian reader, all the papistical captivity, seduction and deceit, wherewith many years the King's true and loving subjects of this his most noble realm of England piteously have been deluded, beguiled and blinded, it should, I think, not only even abhor the ears of all them that be good and virtuous, but also be a labour and burden too great and strange for the learning of him that hath no more than I. . . . Therefore, for this time overpassing so many things without end and reason . . . I shall be content at this time to say my mind in one thing particular, whereof hitherto no man that I know hath anything said or written, for a reformation to be had in the abuse thereof. My meaning is of the crafty juggling, clean conveyance and lewd legerdemain used amongst some men (ye know whom I mean) concerning the impropriations of benefices, of all pestilent infections that ever invaded either realm or region, the most pernicious and diametrically repugnant against the blessed ordinance of Almighty God. . . .

I think no man to be so blind, but he knoweth that Almighty God hath ordained in his faithful congregation of Christian people one special kind of ministers, which are bounden, afore the administration of all sacraments, chiefly and principally to apply themselves to the sincere declaration and publishing of his most holy word and gospel, this witnessing Paul by these words . . . 'The Lord hath not sent me to baptise but rather to preach.' . . . Now if ye grant me that men be bound to labour in the vineyard of the Lord, and in the work of his gospel, I trow and believe that it were not much against good reason that a good workman, and he that laboureth justly for his living had as he is worthy, and as reason and Scripture will, a reward worthy and according to his labour. For the Scripture saith . . . 'A true workman is worthy to have for his work.' And I am sure that the Turk for very shame could not deny this. . . .

I beseech you, all my lords, ladies and masters of impropriations, what other things be your impropriations than things directly fighting against God's holy ordinance, against his holy will, against his most blessed pleasure, against his Holy Spirit. . . . What of him that robbeth a man even at noon in the King's highway, yea, even in the midst of Paul's Church before all men's eyes? Be not you my masters impropriators, suppose ye, even the same persons? . . . Ye shall understand that good and virtuous men before our days, which loved the will of God . . . did . . . for the most easiest way and speediest provision, appoint, assign and ordain (for the same ministers to be maintained) decimations or tithes*, willing and minding by this good provision, that within every congregation or parish the minister of God's word there should be sure at all times of a living. . . . Besides this, they ordained him a mansion to dwell in among them, to the intent that for his diligent administration he should have every thing necessary for him within his own governance; yea, and have it brought even home unto him, to dispose at his pleasure, as it shall be most expedient and necessary for him, that the more quietly he might study and apply himself to minister unto them the pure word of God, and to be ever ready at hand to instruct them of all things necessary for the health of their souls. . . .

Now my masters impropriated or improper masters, how say ye by your fathers, have not you with your crafty collusion almost through England destroyed these holy and godly provisions, made for the maintenance of God's holy word, and for the administration of these most blessed sacraments, for the health, wealth, and salvation of man's soul, for the upholding of the true and Catholic faith, for the supportation of virtue and destruction of vice? Have not you, I say, by the gleeking and gleaning, snatching and scratching, tatching and patching, scraping and raking together of almost all the fat benefices within this realm and impropriating them unto yourselves destroyed this most godly and holy provision, bereaved the people of the true word of God, of the true knowledge of the blessed sacraments, of their true belief and faith in God the Father, and the blood of Jesus Christ?

For how can the people have any faith in God without preaching?

How should they have any preaching when ye have robbed them of their ministers? How should the ministers serve them when ye have robbed them of their living? If the people have no faith, how can they have charity? If they have no charity, what marvel is it, if they run headlong and be carried from one vice to another, from one mischief to another? Be not ye the occasion of all this? Who is else, I pray you? Have not ye the impropriations? Be the impropriations anything else saving benefices, as parsonages, and such like? Do we not say such an abbot is parson here, such a prior is parson here, yea, such a prioress is parson here? How say ye? Think ye that men be fools? Think ye that they be asses? Think ye that they be stocks and stones, blocks and bones? Think ye that we understand no more reason than a great many of you do? Is not this abominable? Is this tolerable?

Is it not great pity to see a man to have three or four benefices; yea, peradventure half a score or a dozen, which he never cometh at, but setteth in every one of them a Sir John Lacklatin, that can scarce read his portas [breviary], or else such a ravening wolf as can do nothing but devour the silly sheep with his false doctrine, and suck their substance from them. Lord, if it be thy pleasure, once have mercy upon us, and give grace that we may have some remedy found for this mischief, both of impropriations and also of them that minister not the word of God faithfully upon their benefices, as they ought to do. For I have known such, that when they have ridden by a benefice whereof they have been parson, they could not tell that it was their benefice. This is a wonderful blindness. And yet I think, such or the same beneficed man will not stick to ride a hundred miles, to prick a brooch upon an image's coat, and think it a right high meritorious deed. But to such time as it shall please the King's most honourable Majesty . . . to see a reformation, as well for the abuse of impropriations as for the uncharitable demeanour of all beneficed men that be not resident and abiding upon their benefices, there to do their bounden duty, it shall never be well in this Church of Christ in England, whereof his Grace is the Supreme Head, nor yet the truth of God's holy word shall ever go forward in his right trade and kind.

Sir Francis Bigod, *A Treatise concernynge Impropriations of Benefices* (c. 1535), reprinted in *Tudor Treatises*, ed. A. G. Dickens (*Yorkshire Archaeological Society, Record Series*, cxxv, 1959), pp. 42-53

II

LATE LOLLARDY AND
EARLY PROTESTANTISM

1 Lollardy on the Eve of the Reformation

In his *Acts and Monuments*, compiled during the 1550s and early 1560s, John
Foxe provides a vast amount of detailed information concerning the survival of
Lollardy throughout the first three decades of the century. To this evidence
much has lately been added from diocesan manuscript-sources wholly or
largely unknown to Foxe. The following is a passage of generalisation by Foxe,
in which he seeks to prove that there was nothing very novel about the Protestant Reformation. From the long list of Lollard heresies he selects, quite
sensibly, 'four principal points': the Lollards' denial of pilgrimages, saint-
worship and transubstantiation*; their reading of the English Scriptures. Their
old manuscript-copies of the latter are mentioned in **6** below. As he claims,
Foxe gleaned a great deal of material from diocesan registers and court books;
in some cases these originals have been lost, in others they survive to support
him. The 'great abjuration' mentioned in the last sentence had been made in
1506 or 1507 by over sixty heretics at Amersham and over twenty at Bucking-
ham.

In turning over the registers and records of Lincoln likewise, and coming to the year of our Lord 1520, and to 1521, I find that as the light of
the Gospel began more to appear, and the number of [its] professors
to grow, so the vehemency of persecution and stir of the bishops began
also to increase; whereupon ensued great perturbation and grievous
affliction in divers and sundry quarters of this realm, especially about
Buckinghamshire and Amersham, Uxbridge, Henley, Newbury, in
the diocese of London, in Essex, Colchester, Suffolk and Norfolk, and
other parts more. And this was before the name of Luther was heard
of in these countries among the people. Wherefore they are much beguiled and misinformed, who condemn this kind of doctrine now

received, of novelty; asking, 'Where was this church and religion forty years ago, before Luther's time?' To whom it may be answered, that this religion and form of doctrine was planted by the Apostles, and taught by true bishops; afterward decayed, and now reformed again....

And if they think this doctrine be so new that it was not heard of before Luther's time, how then came such great persecution before Luther's time here in England? If these were of the same profession which they were of, then was their cruelty unreasonable, so to persecute their own Catholic fraternity. And if they were otherwise, how then is this doctrine of the gospel so new, or how are the professors thereof so late started up as they pretend them to be? But this cometh only of ignorance, and for not knowing nor considering well the times and antiquities of the Church which have been before us; which if they did, they should see and say, that the Church of England hath not lacked great multitudes who tasted and followed the sweetness of God's holy word almost in as ample manner, for the number of well-disposed hearts, as now. Although public authority then lacked to maintain the open preaching of the gospel, yet the secret multitude of true professors was not much unequal; certes the fervent zeal of those Christian days seemed much superior to these our days and times; as manifestly may appear by their sitting up all night in reading and hearing; also by their expenses and charges in buying of books in English, of whom some gave five marks, some more, some less, for a book; some gave a load of hay for a few chapters of *St. James*, or of *St. Paul* in English.

In which rarity of books, and want of teachers, this one thing I greatly marvel and muse at: to note in the registers, and to consider how the word of truth, notwithstanding, did multiply so exceedingly as it did amongst them: wherein is to be seen no doubt the marvellous working of God's mighty power.... To see their travails, their earnest seekings, their burning zeal, their readings, their watchings, their sweet assemblies, their love and concord, their godly living, their faithful demeaning with the faithful, may make us now, in these our days of free profession, to blush for shame.

Four principal points they stood in against the Church of Rome: in pilgrimage, in adoration of saints, in reading Scripture-books in English, and in the carnal presence of Christ's body in the sacrament. After the great abjuration aforesaid, which was under William Smith, Bishop of Lincoln, they were noted and termed among themselves by the name of 'known-men', or 'just-fast-men': as now they are called by the name of Protestants.

Foxe, iv.217-8

2 Thomas Bilney's Conversion

In this letter to Bishop Tunstall of London dated 1527, Thomas Bilney relates his 'conversion' as a result of reading Erasmus's Latin version of the New Testament. The passage suggests that this took place not long after its publication in 1516. Ordained priest in 1519, Bilney did much to create the reforming group in Cambridge, converting both Robert Barnes and Hugh Latimer. A prominent denouncer of saint-worship and an advocate of Tyndale's New Testament, he cannot with any accuracy be termed a Lutheran, even though he stressed Justification by Faith and though his experiences bear some resemblance to those of Luther. He remained orthodox on the Papal Supremacy, the authority of the Church, the doctrines of transubstantiation* and confession. He was nevertheless burned as a relapsed heretic in 1531. See also **3** below.

These men [the persecuting priesthood] do not find pasture, for they never teach and draw others after them, that they should enter by Christ, who alone is the door whereby we must come unto the Father; but set before the people another way, persuading them to come unto God through good works, oftentimes speaking nothing at all of Christ, thereby seeking rather their own gain and lucre than the salvation of souls. . . . These men confess that they know Christ, but by their deeds they deny him.

These are those physicians upon whom a woman that was twelve years vexed with the [issue of blood] had consumed all that she had, and felt no help, but was still worse and worse, until such time as she came at last unto Christ; and after she had once touched the hem of his vesture, through faith she was so healed, that by and by she felt the same in her body [*Luke*, viii.43-8]. O mighty power of the most Highest, which I also, miserable sinner, have often tasted and felt, who, before I could come unto Christ, had even likewise spent all that I had upon those ignorant physicians; that is to say, unlearned hearers of confession; so that there was but small force of strength left in me (who of nature was but weak), small store of money, and very little wit or understanding: for they appointed me fastings, watching, buying of pardons and masses; in all which things (as I now understand) they sought rather their own gain than the salvation of my sick and languishing soul.

But at last I heard speak of Jesus, even then when the New Testament was first set forth by Erasmus, which when I understood to be eloquently done by him, being allured rather by the Latin than by the word of God (for at that time I knew not what it meant), I bought it even by the providence of God, as I do now well understand and perceive: and at the first reading (as I well remember) I chanced upon this sentence of St. Paul (O most sweet and comfortable sentence to my soul!) in *I Timothy*, i: 'It is a true saying, and worthy of all men to be embraced, that Christ Jesus came into the world to save sinners, of whom I am the chief and principal.' This one sentence, through God's instruction and inward working, which I did not then perceive, did so exhilarate my heart, being before wounded with the guilt of my sins, and being almost in despair, that immediately I felt a marvellous comfort and quietness, insomuch that my bruised bones leaped for joy [compare Psalm li.8].

After this, the Scripture began to be more pleasant unto me than the honey or the honey-comb; wherein I learned that all my travails, all my fasting and watching, all the redemption of masses and pardons, being done without trust in Christ, who only saveth his people from their sins; these, I say, I learned to be nothing else but even (as St. Augustine saith) a hasty and swift running out of the right way.

Foxe, iv.635

3 Robert Barnes and the Early Cambridge Reformers

Robert Barnes, prior of the Cambridge Augustinians, was the leading spirit of the discussions held at the White Horse during the earlier 1520s. They were clearly concerned with the new Lutheran theology. During the year 1520 and probably earlier, Luther's books were being read in Cambridge, Oxford and London. Copies were publicly burned in Cambridge about December 1520 and in London at Paul's Cross in May 1521. Most of the future leaders of English Protestantism were in Cambridge during the twenties. Barnes was later active in distributing Tyndale's New Testament (see **6** below). Foxe goes on to describe the arrest, examination and abjuration of Barnes, who subsequently broke penance and escaped to Wittenberg. Barnes returned to England, became one of Thomas Cromwell's agents and suffered martyrdom after Cromwell's fall.

This Barnes, after he came from the university of Louvain, went to Cambridge, where he was made prior and master of the house of the Augustines. At that time the knowledge of good letters was scarcely entered into the university . . . whereupon Barnes, having some feeling of better learning and authors, began in his house to read Terence, Plautus and Cicero, so that what with his industry, pains and labour, and the help of Thomas Parnell, his scholar whom he brought from Louvain with him . . . he caused the house shortly to flourish with good letters. . . . After these foundations laid, then did he read openly in the house Paul's Epistles, and put by Duns and Dorbel [renounced the scholastic authors] . . . and only because he would have Christ there taught, and his holy word, he turned their unsavoury problems and fruitless disputations to other better matter of the holy Scripture; and thereby in short space he made divers good divines. . . . Thus Barnes, what with his reading, disputation and preaching, became famous and mighty in the Scriptures, preaching ever against bishops and hypocrites; and yet did not see his inward and outward idolatry, which he both taught and maintained till that good Master Bilney with others . . . converted him wholly unto Christ.

The first sermon that ever he preached of this truth was the Sunday before Christmas day [1525] at St. Edward's church, belonging to Trinity Hall in Cambridge by the Peas-market, whose theme was the Epistle of the same Sunday, *Gaudete in Domino*, etc.; and so postilled [commented upon] the whole Epistle, following the Scripture and Luther's Postil; and for that sermon he was immediately accused of heresy by two fellows of the King's Hall. Then the godly learned in Christ both of Pembroke Hall, St. John's, Peterhouse, Queen's College, the King's College, Gonville Hall and Benet College showed themselves and flocked together in open sight, both in the schools and at open sermons at St. Mary's and at the Augustines and at other disputations; and then they conferred continually together.

The house that they resorted most commonly unto was the White Horse, which for despite of them, to bring God's word into contempt, was called Germany. This house especially was chosen because many of them of St. John's, the King's College and the Queen's College, came in on the back side. At this time much trouble began to ensue.

Foxe, v.414-5

4   William Tyndale on the Vernacular Bible

Tyndale's first version of the English New Testament was printed in 1525-6 and thereafter secretly shipped in large numbers into England. Tyndale as usual advocates his constructive cause in a bitter anticlerical spirit.

That thou mayest perceive how that the Scripture ought to be in the mother tongue, and that the reasons which our spirits make for the contrary are but sophistry and false wiles to fear thee from the light, that thou mightest follow them blindfold and be their captive to honour their ceremonies and to offer to their belly: first, God gave the children of Israel a law by the hand of Moses in their mother tongue, and all the prophets wrote in their mother tongue, and all the psalms were in the mother tongue. And there was Christ but figured and described in ceremonies, in riddles, in parables and in dark prophecies. What is the cause that we may not have the Old Testament with the New also, which is the light of the Old, and wherein is openly declared before the eyes that which there was darkly prophesied? I can imagine no cause verily, except it be that we should not see the work of Antichrist and juggling of hypocrites. . . .

They will say haply, 'The Scripture requireth a pure mind and a quiet mind: and therefore the layman, because he is altogether cumbered with worldly business, cannot understand them.' If that be the cause, then it is a plain case that our prelates understand not the Scriptures themselves: for no layman is so tangled with worldly business as they are. The great things of the world are ministered by them; neither do the lay people any great thing but at their assignment.

'If the Scripture were in the mother tongue', they will say, 'then would the lay people understand it every man after his own ways.' Wherefore serveth the curate but to teach him the right way? . . . Are ye not abominable schoolmasters in that ye take so great wages, if ye will not teach? If ye would teach, how could ye do it so well and with so great profit as when the lay people have the Scripture before them in their mother tongue? For then should they see, by the order of the text, whether thou jugglest or not. And then would they believe it because it is the Scripture of God, though thy living be never so abominable. . . . But alas, the curates themselves (for the most part) wot no more what the New or Old Testament meaneth than do the Turks. Neither know they of any more than that they read at mass, matins and evensong, which yet they understand not. . . . If they will not let the layman have the word of God in his mother tongue, yet let the priests have it; which, for a great part of them, do understand no Latin at all; but sing and say and patter all day with the lips only that which the heart understandeth not.

> W. Tyndale, *Obedience of a Christian Man* (1528), printed in *Doctrinal Treatises* in *Parker Society*, ed. H. Walker (1848), pp. 144–6

5   Justification by Faith Alone★

These extracts from Tyndale's *Prologue to Romans*, taken from the revised edition (1534) of his New Testament, are perhaps the most important passages in the present book pertaining to the doctrinal Reformation. Tyndale's prologues are only free translations from Luther's, and it was in the following passages that thousands of Englishmen first encountered Luther's key-doctrine of Justification by Faith Alone.

First we must mark diligently the manner of speaking of the Apostle, and above all thing know what Paul meaneth by these words: the Law, Sin, Grace, Faith, Righteousness, Flesh, Spirit and such like, or else read thou it never so oft, thou shalt but lose thy labour. This word Law may not be understand[ed] here after the common manner, and to use Paul's term, after the manner of men or after man's ways: that thou wouldst say the law here in this place were nothing but learning which teacheth what ought to be done, and what ought not to be done, as it goeth with man's law, where the law is fulfilled with outward works only, though the heart be never so far off. But God judgeth the ground of the heart, yea, and the thoughts and the secret movings of the mind, and therefore his law requireth the ground of the heart and love from the bottom thereof, and is not content with the outward work only, but rebuketh those works most of all which spring not of love from the ground and low bottom of the heart, though they appear outward never so honest and good: as Christ in the gospel rebuketh the Pharisees above all other that were open sinners, and calleth them hypocrites, that is to say simulars [counterfeits] and painted sepulchres. Which Pharisees yet lived no men so pure, as pertaining to the outward deeds and works of the law. . . .

The work of the law is: whatsoever a man doeth or can do of his own free will, of his own proper strength and enforcing. Not with standing though there be never so great working, yet as long as there remaineth in the heart unlust [displeasure], tediousness, grudging, grief, pain, loathsomeness and compulsion toward the law, so long are all the works unprofitable, lost, yea and damnable in the sight of God. This meaneth Paul in the third chapter where he sayeth, by the deeds of the law shall no flesh be justified in the sight of God. Hereby perceivest thou that those sophisters are but deceivers, which teach that a man may and must prepare himself to grace and to the favour of God, with good works. . . . Can those works please God thinkest thou, which are done with grief, pain and tediousness, with an evil will, with a contrary and grudging mind? . . .

To fulfil the law is to do the works thereof and whatsoever the law commandeth, with love, lust [pleasure] and inward affection and delectation: and to live godly and well, freely, willingly, and without compulsion of the law, even as though there were no law at all. Such lust and free liberty to love the law cometh only by the working of the Spirit in the heart, as he saith in the first chapter. Now is the Spirit none otherwise given than by faith only, in that we believe the promises of God, without wavering, how that God is true, and will fulfil all his good promises toward us, for Christ's blood's sake. . . . Hereof cometh it that faith only justifieth, maketh righteous, and fulfilleth the law, for it bringeth the Spirit through Christ's deservings [merits]; the Spirit bringeth lust, looseth the heart, maketh him free, setteth him at liberty, and giveth him strength to work the deeds of the law with love, even as the law requireth. Then at the last, out of the same faith so working in the heart, spring all the good works by their own accord. . . .

Faith is not man's opinion and dream, as some imagine and feign when they hear the story of the gospel. . . . But right faith is a thing wrought by the Holy Ghost in us, which changeth us, turneth us into a new nature and begetteth us anew in God, and maketh us the sons of God, as thou readest in the first of *John*, and killeth the old Adam and maketh us altogether new in the heart, mind, will, lust and in all our affections and powers of the soul and bringeth the Holy Ghost with her. Faith is a lively thing, mighty in working, valiant and strong, ever doing, ever fruitful, so that it is impossible that he which is endued therewith should not work all ways good works without ceasing. He asketh not whether good works are to be done or not, but hath done them already ere mention be made of them, and is always doing, for such is his nature now: quick faith in his heart and lively moving of the Spirit drive him and steer him thereunto. Whosoever doeth not good works is an unbelieving person and faithless, and looketh round about groping after faith and good works, and wot not what faith or good works mean, though he babble never so many things of faith and good works.

Faith is then a lively and steadfast trust in the favour of God, wherewith we commit ourselves altogether unto God, and that trust is so surely grounded and sticketh so fast in our hearts, that a man would not once doubt of it, though he should die a thousand times therefore. And such trust wrought by the Holy Ghost through faith maketh a man glad, lusty, cheerful and true-hearted unto God and to all creatures. By the means whereof, willingly and without compulsion he is glad and ready to do good to every man, to do service to every man, to suffer all things, that God may be loved and praised, which hath given him such grace; so that it is impossible to separate good works from faith, even as it is impossible to separate heat and burning from fire. . . .

Righteousness is even such faith, and is called God's righteousness, or righteousness that is of valour [value] before God. For it is God's gift, and it altereth a man and changeth him to a new spiritual nature, and maketh him free and liberal to pay every man his duty. . . . Such righteousness can nature, free will and our own strength never bring to pass. . . .

The sum and whole cause of the writings of this Epistle [to the *Romans*] is to prove that a man is justified by faith only: which proposition whoso denieth, to him is not only this Epistle and all that Paul writeth, but also the whole Scripture so locked up, that he shall never understand it to his soul's health. . . . And by justifying, understand none other thing than to be reconciled to God and to be restored unto his favour, and to have thy sins forgiven thee. As when I say God justifieth us, understand thereby that God for Christ's sake, merits and deservings only, receiveth us unto his mercy, favour and grace, and forgiveth us our sins. . . .

Now go to, reader; and according to the order of Paul's writing, even so do thou.

Farewell
W. T.

The New Testament translated by William Tyndale, 1534 (Cambridge University Press Reprint, 1938, pp. 293-318)

6   Essex Lollards buy Tyndale's Bible

The following is an extract from the confession (1527) of John Tyball, a Lollard from Steeple Bumpstead, Essex. The original uses the alternative spelling 'Barons', but there is no doubt that it was Robert Barnes, who, at the Austin Friars in London, sold Tyndale's New Testament to these visitors and disparaged their old manuscript gospels. With regard to the curate (parish priest) of Bumpstead, it should be noted that the title 'Sir' was commonly accorded to priests.

Furthermore, . . . at Michaelmas last past was twelve month, this respondent [Tyball] and Thomas Hilles came to London to Friar Barnes, then being at the Friars Augustines in London, to buy a New Testament in English, as he saith. And they found the said Friar Barnes in his chamber, whereas there was a merchant man, reading in a book, and two or three more present. And when they came in, the Friar demanded them from whence they came. And they said, from Bumpstead; and so forth in communication they desired the said Friar Barnes that they might be acquainted with him, because they had heard that he was a good man, and because they would have his counsel in the New Testament, which they desired to have of him.

And he [Tyball] saith that the said Friar Barnes did perceive very well that Thomas Hilles and this respondent were infected with opinions, because they would have the New Testament. And then further they showed the said Friar that one Sir Richard Fox, curate of Bumpstead, by their means was well entered in their learning, and said that they thought to get him whole in short space. Wherefore they desired the said Friar Barnes to make a letter to him, that he would continue in that he had begun; which Friar did promise so to write to him a letter at afternoon, and to get them a New Testament.

And then after that communication, the said Thomas Hilles and this respondent showed the Friar Barnes of certain old books that they had; as of four Evangelists, and certain Epistles of Peter and Paul in English, which books the said Friar did little regard, and made a twit of it, and said, 'A point for them, for they be not to be regarded toward [compared with] the new printed Testament in English, for it is of more cleaner English'. And then the said Friar Barnes delivered to them the said New Testament in English, for which they paid 3s. 2d., and desired them that they would keep it close, for he [Barnes] would be loth that it should be known, as he [Tyball] now remembereth. And after the deliverance of the said New Testament to them, the said Friar Barnes did liken the New Testament in Latin to a cimbal tinkling and brass sounding. But what farther exposition he made upon it, he cannot tell. And then at afternoon they fetched the said letter of the said Friar, which he wrote to Sir Richard and read that openly before them; but he doth not now remember what was in the same. And so departed from him, and did never since speak with him, or write to him, as he saith.

J. Strype, *Ecclesiastical Memorials* (1822), vol. i, pt. 2, pp. 54-5

7   A Protestant Merchant outwits a Bishop

This narrative exemplifies the close relationship between the biblical translators and the English merchants in Antwerp, under whose protection Tyndale, Coverdale, Rogers and others worked. It also demonstrates the inability of government and bishops to prevent the massive infiltration of Protestant publications into England. This Bishop of London, Cuthbert Tunstall (1474-1559), was a learned humanist and ambassador and subsequently Bishop of Durham. A Henrician Catholic in the coming crisis, he showed under Mary a marked lack of enthusiasm for persecuting Protestants. The events related below occurred during the summer of 1529, while Tunstall was on the Continent on diplomatic business.

Here is to be remembered that at this present time, William Tyndale had newly translated and imprinted the New Testament in English, and the Bishop of London, not pleased with the translation thereof, debated with himself how he might compass and devise to destroy that false and erroneous translation (as he said). And so it happened that one Augustine Packington, a mercer and merchant of London, and of great honesty, the same time was in Antwerp, where the Bishop then was, and this Packington was a man that highly favoured William Tyndale, but to the Bishop utterly showed himself to the contrary.

The Bishop, desirous to have his purpose brought to pass, communed of the New Testaments, and how gladly he would buy them. Packington then hearing that he wished for, said unto the Bishop, 'My lord, if it be your pleasure, I can in this matter do more, I dare say, than most of the merchants of England that are here, for I know the Dutchmen and strangers that have bought them of Tyndale, and have them here to sell, so that if it be your lordship's pleasure to pay for them (for otherwise I cannot come by them, but I must disburse money for them) I will then assure you to have every book of them, that is imprinted and is here unsold.' The Bishop, thinking that he had God by the toe, when indeed he had (as after he thought) the Devil by the fist, said, 'Gentle Master Packington, do your diligence and get them, and with all my heart I will pay for them, whatsoever they cost you, for the books are erroneous and naughty, and I intend surely to destroy them all, and to burn them at Paul's Cross.' Augustine Packington came to William Tyndale and said, 'William, I know thou art a poor man, and hast a heap of New Testaments and books by thee, for the which thou hast both endangered thy friends and beggared thyself, and I have now gotten thee a merchant, which with ready money shall dispatch thee of all that thou hast, if you think it so profitable for yourself.' 'Who is the merchant?' said Tyndale. 'The Bishop of London', said Packington. 'O, that is because he will burn them', said Tyndale. 'Yea, Mary', quod Packington. 'I am the gladder', said Tyndale, 'for these two benefits shall come thereof; I shall get money of him for these books, to bring myself out of debt, and the whole world shall cry out upon the burning of God's word. And the overplus of the money that shall remain to me shall make me more studious to correct the said New Testament, and so newly to imprint the same once again, and I trust the second will much better like you than ever did the first.'

And so forward went the bargain; the Bishop had the books, Packington the thanks, and Tyndale had the money. Afterwards, when more New Testaments were imprinted, they came thick and threefold into England. The Bishop of London, hearing that still there were so many New Testaments abroad, sent for Augustine Packington and said unto him, 'Sir, how cometh this that there are so many New Testaments abroad, and you promised and assured me that you had bought all?' Then said Packington, 'I promise you I bought all that then was to be had; but I perceive they have made more since, and it will never be better as long as they have the letters and stamps [the type]: therefore it were best for your lordship to buy the stamps too, and then are you sure.' The Bishop smiled at him and said, 'Well, Packington, well.' And so ended this matter.

Edward Hall, Henry VIII (1548), ed. C. Whibley (1904), ii.160-2

8   English Traders in Lutheran Germany

The Lincoln diocesan authorities recorded this examination of Henry Burnett in July 1528. Barrow is on the Lincolnshire coast of the Humber, almost opposite Hull. Simultaneously one of Burnett's shipmates Robert Robinson of Hull was compelled at York to do humiliating penances for his heretical beliefs. The full record suggests that these merchants and sailors acquired only superficial notions of Lutheranism during their stay in German ports, but that they were to some extent imbued with heterodox ideas even before they made this voyage and that they talked incautiously about their experiences when they returned home.

Henry Burnett of Barrow in the county of Lincoln, sworn on the holy gospels of God and thence examined, said that about Candlemas last past [2 February] he and five [men] of Hull, Robert Clarcke, Roger Danyell, Nicholas Bayly and one William [blank] apprentice with Mr. Mycolow of Hull and Robert Robinson of Hull, did pass over the sea in a Dutch ship, freighted with merchandise of Hull, and landed in Holland in a town called Amsterdam; and there they were six or seven weeks, and then took a ship and went to Bremen; and there they freighted a ship with wheat, and they tarried at Bremen five weeks. And there the people did follow Luther's works and no masses were said there, but on the Sunday the priest would revest himself and go to the altar, and proceeded till nigh the sacring time [consecration of the bread and wine], and then the priest and all that were in the church, old and young, would sing after their mother tongue and there was no sacring.

They were at Bremen from Easter till the week afore Whitsunday, and there was none of them houseled [given communion] nor could not be houseled, but they would have been houseled if they could by any means. And they were in divers places of Friesland, and through all the country was there no mass, but after Luther's opinions was the people ordered; and they had every Sunday sermons and preachings, but this respondent [Henry Burnett] nor none of his company did understand them, and in the Whitsun weeks [31 May–6 June] they came to Hull, and there he left his company and came to Barrow. And within four days after, he asked of the vicar of Barrow his curate to be confessed and houseled, and the vicar would neither confess him neither housel him without the consent of his Ordinary*.

Then he was sent to Mr. Doctor Pryn by the commandment of the vicar of Barrow, and Mr. Doctor Pryn sent him to Mr. Chancellor. Interrogated whether he or any of his company went into that country to learn Luther's works or opinions, or no, he saith nay, and they were not nigh Luther, not by fifty Dutch miles. He saith he understandeth no Latin, but he can read English. He had never book of Luther's opinions, but he saith Roger Danyell had the Gospels in English, which the Dean of York hath. He saith that he and his company, in the fish-days, when they were beyond the sea, they did eat fish; and he himself did eat flesh two days [on two fish-days] after he came to Barrow, and never since; and he believeth in God's laws as a good Christian man should do. He was two times at Lincoln to have spoken with Mr. Doctor Pryn for to be houseled, and he went home without any word, for Mr. Doctor Pryn was not at Lincoln.

He was enjoined under pain of the greater excommunication that he shall never teach nor show to any folks such erroneous opinions and damnable abusions as he hath heard and seen in Friesland and the countries thereabout.

Lincoln Diocesan Registry, Cj 4, fos. 16-16v,
printed in *Archaeologia*, xlviii (1885), pp. 257-8

9 The Adventures of Thomas Garret at Oxford

This vivid account of the escape and recapture of the Lutheran scholar and bookseller Thomas Garret was left unfinished by his friend Anthony Dalaber when the latter died in 1562. Foxe completed it from the testimony of 'ancient and credible persons'. Two letters from Dr. London now in the Public Records also report on the matter and are dated 24 and 26 February 1528. Soon afterwards the authorities broke up the Protestant cell at Oxford; three of its members (including John Clark mentioned below) died of disease in a prison at Cardinal College (often described at the time as Frideswide's – later it became Christ Church). Another member John Frith escaped to the Continent: for his later fate see 11 below.

There was great joy and rejoicing among all the papists for [Thomas Garret's] apprehension, and especially with Dr. London, Warden of the New College, and Dr. Higdon, Dean of Frideswide's, two arch-papists, who immediately sent their letters in post-haste unto the Cardinal

[Wolsey] to inform him of the apprehension of this notable heretic; for the which their doing, they were well assured to have great thanks. But of all this sudden hurly-burly was I [Anthony Dalaber] utterly ignorant ... the same week having taken a chamber in Gloucester College, for the purpose of studying the civil law, because the scholars in Alban Hall were all sophisters [second and third year students]. I removed all such poor stuff as I had from thence unto Gloucester College, and there was I much busied in setting up in order my bed, my books, and such things else as I had, so that I had no leisure to go forth anywhere those two days, Friday and Saturday. And having set up all my things handsomely in order the same day before noon, I determined to spend that whole afternoon until evensong time ... at my book in mine own study; and so shut my chamber door unto me, and my study door also, and took into my hand to read Francis Lambert upon the Gospel of *St. Luke*, which book only I had then within there; all my other books written on the Scripture, of which I had great number, as of Erasmus, of Luther, Oecolampadius, etc., I had yet left in my chamber at Alban's Hall, where I had made a very secret place to keep them safe in, because it was so dangerous to have any such books.

[At this point Dalaber was disturbed by furious knocking on his door, and opened it to find Thomas Garret. Having been locked in a college room by the Commissary Dr. Cottesford, Garret had escaped by picking the lock while his captors were at evensong and had hastened to Gloucester College to obtain Dalaber's help in escaping from Oxford.]

But now, with deep sighs and plenty of tears, he prayed me to help to convey him away; and so he cast off his hood and his gown, wherein he came unto me, and desired me to give him a coat with sleeves, if I had any; and told me that he would go into Wales, and thence convey himself into Germany, if he might. Then I put on him a sleeved coat of mine, [of fine cloth in grain, which my mother had given me]. He would also have had another manner of cap of me, but I had none but priestlike, such as his own was. Then kneeled we both down together on our knees, and lifting up our hearts and hands to God, our heavenly Father, desired him, with plenty of tears, so to conduct and prosper him in his journey that he might well escape the danger of all his enemies, to the glory of his holy name, if his good pleasure and will so were. And then we embraced, and kissed the one the other, the tears so abundantly flowing out from both our eyes that we all be-wet both our faces, and scarcely for sorrow could we speak one to the other; and so he departed from me, apparelled in my coat, being committed unto the tuition of our almighty and merciful Father. When he was gone down the stairs from my chamber, I straightways did shut my chamber door, and went into my study, [shutting the door unto me] and taking the New Testament of Erasmus's translation in my hands, kneeled down on my knees, and with many a deep sigh and salt tear, I did with much deliberation read over the tenth chapter of *St. Matthew*'s Gospel; and when I had so done, with fervent prayer I did commit unto God that our dearly beloved brother Garret, earnestly beseeching him ... that he would vouchsafe not only safely to conduct and keep our said dear brother from the hands of all his enemies, but also, that he would endue his tender and lately-born little flock in Oxford with heavenly strength by his holy spirit, that they might be well able thereby valiantly to withstand, to his glory, all their fierce enemies, and also might quietly to their own salvation with all godly patience bear Christ's heavy cross, which I now saw was presently to be laid on their young and weak backs, unable to bear so huge a one without the help of his holy spirit.

This done, I laid aside my book safe, folded up Master Garret's gown and hood and laid them in my press among mine apparel; and so, having put on my short gown, shut up my study and chamber doors and went toward Frideswide's, to speak with that worthy martyr of God, one Master Clark, and others, and to declare unto them what had happened that afternoon.... Then I went straight to Frideswide's, and evensong was begun, and the Dean and the other canons were there in their grey amices; they were almost at *Magnificat* before I came thither. I stood at the choir door and heard Master Taverner play, and others of the chapel there sing, with and among whom I myself was wont to sing also, but now my singing and music was turned into sighing and musing.

As I thus and there stood, in cometh Dr. Cottesford the Commissary as fast as ever he could go, bare-headed and as pale as ashes (I knew his grief well enough); and to the Dean he goeth in the choir, where he was sitting in his stall, and talked with him very sorrowfully: what, I know not, but whereof I might and did well and truly guess. I went aside from the choir door, to see and hear more. The Commissary and Dean came out of the choir wonderfully troubled, as it seemed. About the middle of the church met them Dr. London, puffing, blustering and blowing, like a hungry and greedy lion seeking his prey. They talked together a while, but the Commissary was much blamed of them for keeping of his prisoner so negligently, insomuch that he wept for sorrow.

[Dalaber then relates how he himself was arrested, examined and put in the stocks. Dr. London's letters describe how Dr. Cottesford consulted an astrologer to discover the direction of Garret's flight, and was told that the fugitive had gone to London and 'will shortly to the seaside'. This divination was sensible but, as it happened, wrong. Garret was soon captured by the university proctors at the neighbouring village of Hinksey. Compelled to abjure his heresies, he survived until the fall of Thomas Cromwell in 1540, when he was arrested and burned as a relapsed heretic along with Robert Barnes.]

Foxe, v.422-4

10   Chiltern Lollards hear about Germany

Here we observe a group of Lollards meeting as usual for a Scripture-reading but having as their visiting teacher a Londoner who had recently been in Germany. Nicholas Field's words on the sacrament of the altar suggest Zwinglian rather than Lutheran influence. Foxe says he got these details from the records of Bishop Longland of Lincoln, in which diocese Buckinghamshire lay. We have not located this passage in the surviving Lincoln records, but Foxe is largely vindicated by reference to Longland's Register (Lincoln Reg., xxvi, fo. 180v) which contains a royal writ dated 11 November 1530 for the arrest of some ten named men, among them Nicholas Field and most of those listed by Foxe.

William Wingrave, Thomas Hawks of Hughenden; Robert Hawes of West Wycombe; John Taylor, John Hawks, Thomas Hern of Cobshill; Nicholas Field, Richard Dean, Thomas Clerk the Younger, William Hawks of Chesham; accused A.D. 1530. Persecuted by John Longland, Bishop of Lincoln.

These persons with others were examined, excommunicated, and abjured, for being together in John Taylor's house at Hughenden, and there hearing Nicholas Field of London read a parcel of Scripture in English unto them, who there expounded to them many things; as that they that went on pilgrimage were accursed: that it booted not to pray to images, for they were but stocks made of wood, and could not help a man: that God Almighty biddeth us work as well one day as another, saving the Sunday; for six days he wrought, and the seventh day he rested: that they needed not to fast so many fasting days, except the ember days; for he [Field] was beyond the sea in Almany [Germany], and there they used not so to fast, nor to make such holy days.

Item, that offerings do no good, for they have them, that have no need thereof. And when it was answered again by one, that they maintained God's service: 'Nay', said Nicholas, 'they maintain great houses, as abbeys and others.' Item, that men should say their Paternoster, and Ave Maria in English, with the Creed; and declared the same in English. Item, that the sacrament of the altar was not, as it was pretended, the flesh, blood and bone of Christ, but a sacrament, that is, a typical signification of his holy body.

To William Wingrave moreover it was objected [by the Bishop's judge] that he should say that there was no purgatory*; and if there were any purgatory, and every mass that is said should deliver a soul out of purgatory, there should be never a soul there, for there be more masses said in a day than there be bodies buried in a month.

Foxe, iv.584

11 John Frith on Transubstantiation*

John Frith, educated at Eton and King's College, Cambridge, was among the early Protestant group at Oxford. After his flight (see 9 above) he spent several years at Marburg and was one of Tyndale's collaborators. Very ably, but without vituperation, he attacked Catholic doctrine on purgatory* and on transubstantiation, as he found it expressed in the writings of Fisher and More. Caught and imprisoned soon after his return to England in 1532, he was examined on these two doctrines, and expressed the views on transubstantiation outlined below. As a result, he was burned in 1533. His views were largely inspired by Oecolampadius, the leading Zwinglian writer on the problems of the eucharist. The most interesting aspect of these passages lies, however, in Frith's assertion that transubstantiation was a non-essential, in which men should be left free to believe or to disbelieve. In this limited sense it might be maintained that Frith went to the stake as a champion of religious liberty.

Well, said they [the bishops examining Frith], dost thou not think that his very natural body, flesh, blood and bone, is really contained under the sacrament, and there present without all figure or similitude [not just figuratively]? No, said I, I do not so think: notwithstanding I would not that any should count that i make my saying (which is the negative) any article of faith. For even as I say, that you ought not to make any necessary article of the faith of your part (which is the affirmative), so I say again, that we make no necessary article of the faith of our part, but leave it indifferent for all men to judge therein, as God shall open their hearts, and no side to condemn or despise the other, but to nourish in all things brotherly love; and one to bear another's infirmity. . . . What then is the cause, why I would therefore so willingly suffer death? The cause why I die is this: for that I cannot agree with the divines and other head prelates, that it should be necessarily determined to be an article of faith, and that we should believe, under pain of damnation, the substance of the bread and wine to be changed into the body and blood of our Saviour Jesus Christ, the form and shape only not being changed. Which thing if it were most true (as they shall never be able to prove it by any authority of the Scripture or doctors), yet shall they not so bring to pass, that that doctrine, were it ever so true, should be holden for a necessary article of faith. For there are many things, both in the Scriptures and other places, which we are not bound of necessity to believe as an article of faith. So it is true that I was a prisoner and in bonds when I wrote these things, and yet for all that I will not hold it as an article of faith, but that you may, without danger of damnation, either believe it or think the contrary.

But as touching the cause why I cannot affirm the doctrine of transubstantiation, divers reasons do lead me thereunto: first, for that I do plainly see it to be false and vain, and not to be grounded upon any reason, either of the Scriptures, or of approved doctors. Secondly, for that by my example I would not be an author unto Christians to admit anything as a matter of faith, more than the necessary points of their creed, wherein the whole sum of our salvation doth consist, especially such things, the belief whereof hath no certain argument of authority or reason. I added moreover that their Church (as they call it) hath no such power and authority, that it either ought or may bind us, under the peril of our souls to be believing of such articles. Thirdly, because I will not, for the favour of our divines or priests, be prejudicial in this point unto so many nations, of Germans, Helvetians and others, which, altogether rejecting the transubstantiation of the bread and wine into the body and blood of Christ, are all of the same opinion that I am, as well those that take Luther's part, as those that hold with Oecolampadius.

Which things standing in this case, I suppose there is no man of any upright conscience, who will not allow the reason of my death, which I am put unto for this only cause, that I do not think transubstantiation, although it were true indeed, to be established for an article of faith.

Foxe, v.12-14, reprinted from *A Boke made by Johan Fryth, prysoner in the Tour of London* (A. Scoloker, 1548)

III

THE HENRICIAN
REFORMATION, 1531-6

Documents 1-10 in this Section have at their root the erastian* principle first explicitly stated in the preamble to the Act in Restraint of Appeals, 1533 (5): namely, that the commonwealth or 'body politic' consists of two parts, the 'spiritualty' and the 'temporalty'; that the members of both are equally subjects of 'this realm of England [which] is an empire'; and that consequently the members of both are equally under the authority of the 'Supreme Head and King', who has been invested directly by God with complete power to rule and to render justice both spiritual and temporal, without recourse to any foreign authority.

Not all the relevant Acts are printed here but references to those excluded (e.g. Acts of Succession and Treason) will be found in the course of the Section.

Documents 1, 2, 3 and 9 deal primarily with the question of 'internal' relations between King Henry VIII and the English clergy: 4, 5, 6 and 7, whilst having an all-important bearing on these relations, are primarily concerned with the progressive severance of ties with Rome: 8 and 10 could be said to cover both these matters. In 11, Thomas More seeks to refute the principle underlying 1-10. It will be seen that Henry had already established his supremacy over the English clergy before the anti-papal legislation began. The latter becomes increasingly aggressive in tone as time goes by. We have already observed that the Henrician Reformation cannot be equated with a Protestant Reformation. The wording in two Acts (4 (preamble)) and 7 (§ XIII) testifies to this. Even more important in this connection is 10 below: a trenchant exposition by a staunchly conservative, anti-Protestant and very able bishop of the erastian concept mentioned above.

Henry VIII's own doctrinal position was as orthodox as Gardiner's and is truly reflected in the statement in 7 that the King and realm do not intend to 'vary from the congregation of Christ's Church in any things concerning the very articles of the Catholic faith of Christendom'. For further detail about doctrinal and disciplinary matters up to 1539, see IV below.

I   Act for the Pardon of the Clergy, 1531 (22 Hen. VIII, c. 15)

The determination of the 'temporalty' to curtail the privileges of the 'spiritualty' had clearly expressed itself in the first session of the Reformation Parliament in 1529 (see **I, 3**). In 1530 and 1531 the process was taken much further when the imposition of effective royal controls began. Indictments under *Praemunire**** were brought, first against Cardinal Wolsey, then against fifteen other prominent divines, and finally against the whole of the English clergy. Broadly speaking, these various charges denied the right of any English cleric—high or low—to exercise any form of ecclesiastical jurisdiction in the King's dominions without royal permission.

The final result was the Act below. The 'subsidy' of £100,000 really amounted to a fine, by which the province of Canterbury bought the King's pardon. A similar Act (23 Hen. VIII, c. 19) covered the much less wealthy province of York, from which a payment of £18,840 was required.

In the same year (1531) Henry obtained from the clergy an acknowledgment that he was the 'Protector and Supreme Head of the English Church and Clergy', though at this stage the clergy insisted on the important addition 'so far as the law of Christ allows'. Later, as the clergy became more submissive, this saving clause was dropped: it is not included in the Act forbidding Papal Dispensations (**7** below) or in the Act of Supremacy (**8** below).

The King, our Sovereign Lord, calling to his blessed and most gracious remembrance that his good and loving subjects the most reverend father in God the Archbishop of Canterbury [Warham] and other bishops, suffragans, prelates and other spiritual persons of the province of the archbishopric of Canterbury ... and the ministers ... which have exercised, practised or executed in spiritual courts and other spiritual jurisdictions within the said province, have fallen and incurred into divers dangers of his laws by things done, perpetrated and committed contrary to the order of his laws, and specially contrary to the form of the Statutes of Provisors****, Provisions and *Praemunire*; and his Highness, having alway tender eye with mercy and pity and compassion towards his said spiritual subjects, minding of his high goodness and great benignity so always to impart the same unto them as justice being daily administered all rigour be excluded, and the great and benevolent minds of his said subjects largely and many times approved towards his Highness, and specially in their Convocation and Synod now presently being in the chapter house of the monastery of Westminster, by correspondence of gratitude to them to be requited: of

his mere motion, benignity and liberality, by authority of this his Parliament, hath given and granted his liberal and free pardon to his said
good and loving spiritual subjects . . . to be had, taken and enjoyed to
and by them and every of them by virtue of this present Act. . . . [The
pardon is granted 'in consideration that' the province of Canterbury
in their Convocation have agreed to give the King a subsidy of
£100,000.]

*   *   *

Stat. Realm, iii.334-8

2   The Supplication of the Commons against the Ordinaries*, 1532

This Supplication was originally drafted by Thomas Cromwell in 1529. In 1532
it was presented to the King in a revised form. It is difficult to know whether by
now the main impetus sprang from the Commons (as the title would suggest)
or from the government, but there can be little doubt that the contents of the
Supplication truly reflected lay animosity.
The clergy sent an 'Answer' to the Supplication in which they maintained that
since the making of canons was a duty prescribed by God, they could not
promise to submit their making to the King. They rejected the wholesale
charges made against themselves whilst offering to look into any particular
defaults if full details were forthcoming. They asserted that physical violence
was offered by 'ill-disposed and seditious persons' to some members of their
calling, who are 'thrown down in the kennel [gutter] in the open street at mid-
day, even here within your own city', and they ended with a plea for the
King's protection.
In this portentous altercation between 'spiritualty' and 'temporalty' the King
himself intervened so effectively that the result was the total collapse of clerical
resistance and the 'Submission' on 15 May 1532 (3 below). With this the King
was satisfied, and any hopes which the laity may have entertained for the
complete abolition or overhaul of ecclesiastical courts were disappointed (see
Introduction, p. 6).

*   *   *

First, the prelates and other of the clergy of this your realm, being your
subjects, in their Convocation by them holden . . . have made and daily
make divers fashions of laws and ordinances concerning temporal
things; and some of them be repugnant to the laws and statutes of your

realm; not having ne requiring your most royal assent to the same laws by them so made, nor any assent or knowledge of your lay subjects is had to the same, nor to them published and known in the English tongue. . . . Declaring the infringers of the same laws so by them made not only to incur into the terrible censures of excommunication but also unto the detestable crime and sin of heresy; by the which divers of your most humble and obedient lay subjects be brought into this ambiguity whether they may do and execute your laws according to your jurisdiction royal of this your realm for dread of the same pains and censures comprised in the said laws. . . .

Also divers and many of your said most humble and obedient subjects, and specially those that be of the poorest sort . . . be daily convented and called before the said spiritual ordinaries, their commissaries and substitutes, *ex officio*, sometime at the pleasures of the said ordinaries . . . for displeasure without any provable cause, and sometime at the only promotion and suggestion of their summoners . . . being very light and indiscreet persons . . . and sometime . . . at the only will and pleasure of the ordinaries . . . they be committed to prison without bail . . . and there some lie, as it is reported, half a year and some more [before] they can come to their declaration. . . . Divers so appearing . . . shall be constrained to answer to many subtle questions and interrogatories only invented and exhibited at the pleasure of the said ordinaries . . . by the which a simple, unlearned or else a well-witted layman without learning sometime is and commonly may be trapped and induced by an ignorant answer to the peril of open penance to his shame; or else to redeem the same penance for money, as it is commonly used. . . .

Also divers and many your most humble and obedient lay subjects be originally cited to appear out of the diocese that they dwell in, and many times be suspended and excommunicate for small and light causes. . . .

Also your said most humble and obedient subjects find themselves grieved with the great and excessive fees taken in the . . . spiritual courts. . . . Also in probate of testaments, notwithstanding the last statutes thereof made [see **I, 3**], there is invented new fashions to charge your subjects for probate of testaments . . . long delays . . . or the proof thereof can be admitted. . . . And likewise since the statute made for mortuaries [see **I, 3**], there is exacted and demanded of your

subjects in divers parishes of this your realm other manner of tithes*
than they have been accustomed to pay this hundreds of years past. . . .

And also, whereas divers spiritual persons, being presented as well by
your Highness as by other patrons . . . to divers benefices . . . the said
ordinaries and their ministers do not only take of them for their letters
of institution and induction many great and large sums of money and
rewards, but also do long delay them without reasonable cause before
they will admit, institute and induct them, because they will have the
profits of the benefice during vacation, unless they will pact and
covenant with them by temporal bonds . . . whereof some bonds contain that the ordinaries should have part of the profits of the said
benefice after their institution. . . .

And also the said spiritual ordinaries do daily confer and give sundry
benefices unto certain young folks, calling them their nephews or kins-
folk, being in their minority . . . apt ne able to serve the cure of any
such benefice; whereby the said ordinaries do keep and detain the
fruits and profits of the same benefices in their own hands . . . and the
poor silly [simple] souls of your people and subjects . . . for lack of
good curates do perish without good example, doctrine or any good
teaching.

*   *   *

Public Record Office, S.P.6 / I, no. 22

3   The Submission of the Clergy, 1532

See 2 above. The day after this 'Submission' Sir Thomas More pleaded ill-
health and resigned the Chancellorship.
In 1534 an Act for the Submission of the Clergy to the King's Majesty (25
Hen. VIII, c. 19) gave statutory confirmation to the following Submission of
1532, and enacted that the special commission of 32 persons requested by the
clergy to review all canons should be set up. This commission was not in fact
appointed.

We your most humble subjects, daily orators and beadsmen of your
clergy of England, having our special trust and confidence in your most
excellent wisdom, your princely goodness and fervent zeal to the
promotion of God's honour and Christian religion, and also in your
learning, far exceeding, in our judgment, the learning of all other kings

and princes that we have read of, and doubting nothing but that the same shall still continue and daily increase in your Majesty:

First, do offer and promise, *in verbo sacerdotii*, here unto your Highness, submitting ourselves most humbly to the same, that we will never from henceforth enact . . . or execute any new canons or constitutions provincial, or any other new ordinance, provincial or synodal, in our Convocation or Synod in time coming, which Convocation is, alway hath been, and must be, assembled only by your Highness's commandment of writ, unless your Highness by your royal assent shall license us to assemble our Convocation, and to . . . execute such constitutions . . . and thereto give your royal assent and authority.

Secondly, that whereas divers of the constitutions [etc.] . . . which have been heretofore enacted, be thought to be not only much prejudicial to your prerogative royal, but also overmuch onerous to your Highness's subjects, your clergy aforesaid is contented, if it may stand so with your Highness's pleasure, that it be committed to the examination and judgment of your Grace and of thirty-two persons, whereof sixteen to be of the upper and nether house of the temporalty [Houses of Lords and Commons], and other sixteen of the clergy, all to be chosen and appointed by your most noble Grace. So that, finally, whichsoever of the said constitutions [etc.] . . . shall be thought and determined by your Grace and by the most part of the said thirty-two persons not to stand with God's laws and the laws of your realm, the same to be abrogated and taken away by your Grace and the clergy; and such of them as shall be seen by your Grace and by the most part of the said thirty-two persons, to stand with God's laws and the laws of your realm, to stand in full strength and power, your Grace's most royal assent and authority once . . . fully given to the same.

Public Record Office, S.P.1/70, pp. 35-6

4 Act in Conditional Restraint of Annates★ and concerning the Consecration of Bishops, 1532 (23 Hen. VIII, c. 20)

Annates (or first fruits★ as defined up to 1533) were the payments claimed by the pope and papal curia from the first year's revenue of a new benefice in certain cases: chiefly affected were clerics appointed to archbishoprics and bishoprics, who paid large sums to Rome. The preamble to this Act does not,

however, reflect the true situation. Between 1485 and 1533 payments made to
Rome by the English Church (including annates) averaged about £4,800
annually, whereas during the same period, payments by the English Church to
the Crown in taxation of various kinds amounted to about £12,500 annually.
An important consequence of the threat contained in § II of the Act was the
dispatch by Rome early in 1533 of the necessary bulls for the consecration of
Thomas Cranmer as Archbishop of Canterbury.
In regard to § IV it should be noted that letters patent dated 9 July 1533 declared that the Act should stand. In 1534 annates were withheld from Rome
absolutely (6 below), on the ground that the 'gentle courtesy and friendly ways'
envisaged in § III had been disregarded by the Pope. Later in the same year
these same payments were annexed to the Crown, first fruits being then defined
as the whole of one year's clear income (9 below).

Forasmuch as it is well perceived, by long-approved experience, that
great and inestimable sums of money [have] been daily conveyed out
of this realm, to the impoverishment of the same; and specially such
sums of money as the Pope's Holiness, his predecessors, and the Court
of Rome, by long time have heretofore taken of all and singular those
spiritual persons which have been named, elected, presented, or postulated to be archbishops or bishops within this realm of England, under
the title of annates, otherwise called first fruits: which annates, or first
fruits, heretofore have been taken of every archbishopric or bishopric
within this realm, by restraint of the Pope's bulls, for confirmations,
elections, admissions, postulations, provisions, collations, dispositions,
institutions, installations, investitures, orders, holy benedictions, palls,
or other things requisite and necessary to the attaining of those their
promotions; and have been compelled to pay, before they could attain
the same, great sums of money.... And for because the said annates
have risen, grown, and increased, by an uncharitable custom, grounded
upon no just or good title, ... and [are] taken by constraint, against
all equity and justice:

The noblemen, therefore, of this realm, and the wise, sage, politic
Commons of the same, assembled in this present Parliament, considering that the Court of Rome ceaseth not to tax, take, and exact the said
great sums of money, under the title of annates, or first fruits, as is
aforesaid, to the great damage of the said prelates and this realm; which
annates, or first fruits, were first suffered to be taken within the same
realm, for the only defence of Christian people against the infidels, and
now they be claimed and demanded as mere duty, only for lucre,

against all right and conscience: insomuch that it is evidently known, that there hath passed out of this realm unto the Court of Rome, since the second year of the reign of the most noble prince of famous memory, King Henry VII, unto this present time, under the name of annates, or first fruits, paid for the expedition of bulls of archbishoprics and bishoprics, the sum of eight hundred thousand ducats, amounting in sterling money, at the least, to eight score thousand pounds, besides other great and intolerable sums which have yearly been conveyed to the said Court of Rome, by many other ways and means, to the great impoverishment of this realm:

And albeit that our said Sovereign Lord the King, and all his natural subjects, as well spiritual as temporal, be as obedient, devout, catholic, and humble children of God and holy Church, as any people be within any realm christened; yet the said exactions of annates, or first fruits, be so intolerable and importable [unbearable] to this realm, that it is considered and declared, by the whole body of this realm now represented by all the estates of the same assembled in this present Parliament, that the King's Highness before Almighty God is bound, as by the duty of a good Christian prince, for the conservation and preservation of the good estate and commonwealth of this his realm, to do all that in him is to obviate, repress, and redress the said abusions and exactions of annates, or first fruits: . . .

It is therefore ordained, established, and enacted, by authority of this present Parliament, that the unlawful payments of annates, or first fruits, and all manner contributions for the same, for any archbishopric or bishopric, or for any bulls hereafter to be obtained from the Court of Rome, to or for the aforesaid purpose and intent, shall from henceforth utterly cease, and no such hereafter to be paid for any archbishopric or bishopric within this realm, other or otherwise than hereafter in this present Act is declared; and that no manner person nor persons hereafter to be named, elected, presented, or postulated to any archbishopric or bishopric within this realm, shall pay the said annates, or first fruits, for the said archbishopric or bishopric, nor any other manner of sum or sums of money, pensions, or annuities for the same, or for any other like exaction, or cause, upon pain to forfeit to our said Sovereign Lord the King, his heirs and successors, all manner his goods and chattels for ever, and all the temporal lands and possessions of the same archbishopric or bishopric. . . .

[II   If the Court of Rome should deny or delay the requisite bulls for
the consecration of any prelate hereafter presented by the Crown, then
he is to be consecrated without them; if a bishop, 'by the archbishop
in whose province the said bishopric shall be', and if an archbishop, by
two bishops appointed by the King.]

III   And to the intent our said Holy Father the Pope, and the Court of
Rome shall not think that the pains and labours . . . taken about the
writing [and] sealing . . . of any bulls hereafter to be obtained or had
for any such archbishopric or bishopric shall . . . not be sufficiently . . .
recompensed in that behalf; and for their more ready expedition to be
had therein: it is therefore enacted . . . that every spiritual person of
this realm, hereafter to be . . . presented . . . to any archbishopric or
bishopric of this realm, shall and may lawfully pay for the writing and
obtaining of his . . . bulls, at the Court of Rome, and ensealing the
same with lead, to be had without payment of any annates . . . five
pounds sterling . . . for the clear yearly value of every hundred pounds
of every such archbishopric or bishopric and not above. . . .

And forasmuch as the King's Highness, and this his High Court of
Parliament, neither have, nor do intend to use in this, or any other like
cause, any manner of extremity or violence, before gentle courtesy
and friendly ways and means first approved and attempted . . . have
therefore thought convenient to commit the final order and determination of the premises, in all things, unto the King's Highness. So
that if it may seem to his high wisdom, and most prudent discretion,
meet to move the Pope's Holiness, and the Court of Rome, amicably,
charitably and reasonably to compound, either to extinct . . . the payments of the said annates . . . or else, by some friendly, loving and
tolerable composition, to moderate the same, in such wise as may be
by this his realm easily borne and sustained: that then those ways and
compositions once . . . agreed, between the Pope's Holiness and the
King's Highness, shall stand in strength, force and effect of a law, inviolably to be observed.

[IV   The King shall declare by his letters patent before the next
Parliament whether or not the 'premises or any part' thereof shall take
effect as a statute.

V   If reasonable means of determination fail, and the Pope attempts
excommunication or interdict, any such sentence shall have no effect

and the King and his lay subjects may 'without any scruple of conscience' continue to enjoy all the sacraments and divine services of the Church.]

Stat. Realm, iii.385-8

5 Act in Restraint of Appeals, 1533 (24 Hen. VIII, c. 12)

In January 1533 Henry had been secretly married to Anne Boleyn. The immediate aim of the following Act, passed in February 1533, was to provide that Henry's divorce case – now urgent since Anne Boleyn was known to be pregnant – should be determined by a special court presided over by Cranmer. As observed, the long-term consequences of the Act were much wider, indeed momentous.

The references in the preamble to statutes made in earlier times are mainly to the Statutes of Provisors★ and *Praemunire*★. In the later Act for the Submission of the Clergy, 1534 (see **3** above), the provisions of the following Act concerning the course of appeals were strengthened as follows:

(i) their scope was widened to include not only specified causes such as matrimony, divorce, etc., but all causes;

(ii) final appeal could be made beyond the archiepiscopal courts: in fact to the King in Chancery.

Where by divers sundry old authentic histories and chronicles, it is manifestly declared and expressed, that this realm of England is an empire, and so hath been accepted in the world, governed by one Supreme Head and King, having the dignity and royal estate of the imperial Crown of the same, unto whom a body politic, compact of all sorts and degrees of people, divided in terms, and by names of spiritualty and temporalty, be bounden and owe to bear, next to God, a natural and humble obedience: he being also institute and furnished, by the goodness and sufferance of Almighty God, with plenary, whole, and entire power, pre-eminence, authority, prerogative and jurisdiction, to render and yield justice, and final determination to all manner of folk, residents, or subjects within his realm, in all causes, matters, debates, and contentions, happening to occur, insurge, or begin within the limits thereof, without restraint or provocation to any foreign princes or potentates of the world: the body spiritual whereof having power, when any cause of the law divine happened to come in question, or of spiritual learning, then it was declared, interpreted, and showed by that part of the said body politic, called the spiritualty, now being usually called the English Church, which always hath been reputed ... both for knowledge [and] integrity ..., sufficient and meet of itself, without the intermeddling of any exterior person or persons, to declare and determine all such doubts, and to administer all such offices and duties, as to their rooms spiritual doth appertain; for the due administration whereof, and to keep them from corruption and sinister affection, the King's most noble progenitors, and the antecessors of the nobles of this realm, have sufficiently endowed the said Church, both with honour and possessions; and the laws temporal, for trial of propriety of lands and goods, and for the conservation of the people of this realm in unity and peace, without ravin or spoil, was and yet is administered, adjudged, and executed by sundry judges and ministers of the other part of the said body politic, called the temporalty; and both their authorities and jurisdictions do conjoin together in the due administration of justice, the one to help the other.

And whereas the King, his most noble progenitors, and the nobility and Commons of this said realm, at divers and sundry Parliaments, as well in the time of King Edward I, Edward III, Richard II, Henry IV, and other noble kings of this realm, made sundry ordinances, laws, statutes, and provisions for the entire and sure conservation of the prerogatives, liberties, and pre-eminences of the said imperial Crown of this realm, and of the jurisdictions spiritual and temporal of the same, to keep it from the annoyance as well of the see of Rome, as from the authority of other foreign potentates, attempting the diminution or violation thereof. ...

And notwithstanding the said good statutes ... sundry inconveniences and dangers, not provided for plainly by the said former acts, statutes and ordinances, have risen and sprung by reason of appeals sued out of this realm to the see of Rome, in causes testamentary, causes of matrimony and divorces, right of tithes,* oblations [things assigned to pious uses] and obventions [fees occasionally received], not only to the great inquietation, vexation, trouble, costs and charges of the King's Highness, and many of his subjects ... but also to the great delay and let [hindrance] to the true and speedy determination of the said causes ...:

And forasmuch as the great distance of way is so far out of this realm, so that the necessary proofs, nor the true knowledge of the cause, can neither there be so well known, nor the witnesses there so well examined, as within this realm, so that the parties grieved by means of the said appeals be most times without remedy:

In consideration whereof the King's Highness, his nobles and Commons, considering the great enormities, dangers, long delays and hurts, that as well to his Highness, as to his said nobles, subjects, commons, and residents of this his realm, in the said causes . . . do daily ensue, doth therefore by his royal assent, and by the assent of the Lords spiritual and temporal and the Commons in this present Parliament assembled, and by the authority of the same, enact, establish, and ordain, that all [such] causes . . . shall be from henceforth heard, examined, discussed, clearly, finally, and definitively adjudged and determined within the King's jurisdiction and authority, and not elsewhere, in such courts spiritual and temporal of the same, as the natures, conditions, and qualities of the causes . . . shall require . . . any foreign inhibitions, appeals, sentences . . . interdictions, excommunications, restraints, judgments, or any other process . . . from the see of Rome, or any other foreign courts or potentates of the world . . . notwithstanding. . . . As also, that all the spiritual prelates, pastors, ministers and curates within this realm, and the dominions of the same, shall and may use, minister, execute and do . . . all sacraments, sacramentals, divine services and all other things within the said realm and dominions unto all the subjects of the same as catholic and Christian men owe to do; any former . . . interdictions, excommunications or appeals . . . not-withstanding. . . .

[II   Any person attempting to obtain from Rome or any other foreign court an appeal or judgment, or in any way contravening the provisions of this Act, will incur penalties under the Statutes of *Praemunire* and Provisors.

III   sets out the exact 'manner and form' in which the King's subjects shall henceforth take appeals for determination. The courts of final appeal are to be the Archbishops' courts.

IV   In any 'matter or contention' which 'may touch the King' appeal shall lie to the Upper House of Convocation for final determination.]

Stat. Realm, iii.427-9

6   Act in Absolute Restraint of Annates* and concerning the Election of Bishops, 1534 (25 Hen. VIII, c. 20)

See **4** above and **9** below. The following Act not only withheld annates absolutely, but laid down the procedure to be followed in the election of bishops. It is interesting to note that with the exception of alterations in the reigns of Edward VI (see **VII, 1**) and Mary this procedure – restored in 1559 – has continued to the present day. The 'licence under the great seal' referred to in § III is generally known as the *'congé d'élire'*. Before the Dissolution seven cathedrals had monastic chapters: hence the reference in § III to 'the prior and convent, or the dean and chapter'. After the Dissolution such chapters were replaced by deans and secular canons. Often these were the former abbots, priors and monks.

[§ I begins by reciting the Act for the Conditional Restraint of Annates – **4** above.] And albeit the said Bishop of Rome, otherwise called the Pope, hath been informed and certified of the effectual contents of the said Act, to the intent that by some gentle ways the said exactions might have been redressed and reformed, yet nevertheless the said Bishop of Rome hitherto hath made none answer of his mind therein to the King's Highness, nor devised or required any reasonable ways to and with our said Sovereign Lord for the same:

Wherefore his most Royal Majesty of his most excellent goodness, for the wealth and profit of this his realm and subjects of the same, hath not only put his most gracious and royal assent to the aforesaid Act, but also hath ratified and confirmed the same and every clause and article therein contained, as by his letters patents under his great seal enrolled in the Parliament roll of this present Parliament more at large is contained.

II   And forasmuch as in the said Act it is not plainly and certainly expressed in what manner and fashion archbishops and bishops shall be elected, presented, invested and consecrated within this realm . . .; be it now therefore enacted . . . that the said Act and everything therein contained shall be and stand in strength, virtue and effect; except only, that no person . . . hereafter shall be presented, nominated, or commended to the said Bishop of Rome . . . for the dignity or office of any archbishop or bishop within this realm, or in any other the King's dominions, nor shall send . . . there for any manner of bulls . . . or other things requisite for an archbishop or bishop, nor shall pay any sums of money for annates . . . or otherwise for expedition of any such bulls . . .; but that by the authority of this Act, such presenting, nominating or commending to the said Bishop of Rome . . . and such bulls . . . annates, first fruits* and every other sums of money hereto-fore . . . paid at the said see of Rome . . . shall utterly cease. . . .

III And furthermore be it ordained and established . . . that at every avoidance [vacancy] of every archbishopric or bishopric within this realm, or in any other the King's dominions, the King our Sovereign Lord, his heirs and successors, may grant unto the prior and convent, or the dean and chapter of the cathedral churches or monasteries where the see of such archbishopric or bishopric shall happen to be void, a licence under the great seal, as of old time hath been accustomed, to proceed to election of an archbishop or bishop of the see so being void, with a letter missive, containing the name of the person which they shall elect and choose: by virtue of which licence the said dean and chapter, or prior and convent, to whom any such licence and letters missives shall be directed, shall with all speed and celerity in due form elect and choose the said person named in the said letters missives, to the dignity and office of the archbishopric or bishopric so being void, and none other.

And if they do defer or delay their election above twelve days next after such licence and letters missives to them delivered, that then for every such default the King's Highness, his heirs and successors, at their liberty and pleasure shall nominate and present, by their letters patents under their great seal, such a person to the said office and dignity so being void, as they shall think able and convenient for the same. . . .

* * *

[VI If a dean and chapter, or prior and convent, 'proceed not to election' after receiving the licence, or if any archbishop or bishops refuse to consecrate and invest any prelate duly elected – in each case 'within twenty days next' after the appropriate notice 'shall come to their hands' – then they shall 'run into the dangers . . . and penalties' of *Praemunire**.]

Stat. Realm, iii.462-4

7   Act forbidding Papal Dispensations* and Payment of Peter's Pence, 1534 (25 Hen. VIII, c. 21.)

Dispensations were licences allowing departures from the canon law, e.g. a licence to hold more than one benefice. Peter's Pence, begun centuries earlier as a papal levy of 1d. a year on most households, had been long since compounded for a fixed annual payment to the pope of just under £200.

The following Act firmly and categorically puts great ecclesiastical powers into the hands of the King. Royal predominance is stressed by the limitations imposed on the Archbishop's powers of dispensation and by the proposed royal visitation of monasteries and other institutions previously exempt from episcopal visitation.

Several further Acts of Parliament consolidated Henry's position:

(i)   The Act of Supremacy, 1534 (8 below), accepted the King's supremacy as a fact but gave him more positive powers to define doctrine and to discipline the 'spiritualty' in any way he personally deemed necessary. It will be noted that it includes no legal sanctions. These were provided in the following Acts.

(ii)   The Treason Act, 1534 (26 Hen. VIII, c. 13), declared that from 1 February 1535 it would be high treason to deprive the King and Queen and their heirs 'of the dignity, title, or name of their royal estates, or slanderously and maliciously [to] publish and pronounce, by express writing or words, that the King our Sovereign Lord should be heretic, schismatic, tyrant, infidel or usurper of the Crown'.

(iii)   The Act of Succession, 1534 (25 Hen. VIII, c. 22), and its completion in a further Act (26 Hen. VIII, c. 2) made it treason to slander Henry's marriage with Anne Boleyn, or to refuse to take the oath upholding the 'whole effects and contents' of the Act. Further Acts of Succession protected by treason clauses each of Henry's wives and the succession.

(iv)   The Act extinguishing the Authority of the Bishop of Rome, 1536 (28 Hen. VIII, c. 10), re-emphasised the penalties involved in maintaining the authority of the Pope.

Most humbly beseeching your most Royal Majesty, your obedient and faithful subjects, the Commons of this your present Parliament assembled, by your most dread commandment, that where your subjects of this your realm, and of other countries and dominions, being under your obeisance, by many years past have been, and yet be greatly decayed and impoverished, by such intolerable exactions of great sums of money as have been claimed and taken, and yet continually be claimed to be taken out of this your realm, and other your said countries and dominions, by the Bishop of Rome, called the Pope, and the see of Rome, as well in pensions, censes [taxes], Peter's Pence, procurations, fruits, suits for provisions and expeditions of bulls for archbishoprics and bishoprics and for ... dispensations, licences, faculties, ... and other infinite sorts of bulls, briefs, and instruments of sundry natures, names, and kinds in great numbers heretofore practised and obtained otherwise than by the laws, laudable uses, and customs of this realm should be permitted, the specialties whereof be over long, large in number and tedious here particularly to be inserted; wherein the Bishop of Rome aforesaid hath not been only to be blamed for his usurpation in the premises, but also for his abusing and beguiling your subjects, pretending and persuading to them that he hath full power to dispense with all human laws, uses, and customs of all realms, in all causes which be called spiritual, which matter hath been usurped and practised by him and his predecessors by many years, in great derogation of your imperial Crown and authority royal, contrary to right and conscience:

For where this your Grace's realm recognising no superior under God, but only your Grace, hath been and is free from subjection to any man's laws, but only to such as have been devised, made, and ordained within this realm, for the wealth of the same, or to such other as, by sufferance of your Grace and your progenitors, the people of this your realm have taken at their free liberty, by their own consent to be used amongst them, and have bound themselves by long use and custom to the observance of the same, not as to the observance of the laws of any foreign prince, potentate, or prelate, but as to the accustomed and ancient laws of this realm, originally established as laws of the same, by the said sufferance, consents, and custom, and none otherwise:

It standeth therefore with natural equity and good reason, that in all and every such laws human made within this realm, or induced into this realm by the said sufferance, consents, and custom, your Royal Majesty, and your Lords spiritual and temporal, and Commons, representing the whole state of your realm, in this your most High Court of Parliament, have full power and authority, not only to dispense, but also to authorise some elect person or persons to dispense with those, and all other human laws of this your realm, and with every one of them, as the quality of the persons and matter shall require; and also the said laws, and every one of them, to abrogate, annul, amplify, or diminish, as it shall be seen unto your Majesty, and the nobles and

Commons of your realm present in your Parliament, meet and convenient. . . .

And because that it is now in these days present seen, that the state, dignity, superiority, reputation, and authority of the said imperial Crown of this realm, by the long sufferance of the said unreasonable and uncharitable usurpations and exactions practised in the times of your most noble progenitors, is much and sore decayed and diminished, and the people of this realm thereby impoverished, and so or worse be like to continue, if remedy be not therefor shortly provided:

It may therefore please your most noble Majesty, for the honour of Almighty God, and for the tender love, zeal, and affection that ye bear, and always have borne to the wealth of this your realm and subjects of the same, forasmuch as your Majesty is Supreme Head of the Church of England, as the prelates and clergy of your realm, representing the said Church, in their Synods and Convocations have recognised, in whom consisteth full power and authority, upon all such laws as have been made and used within this realm, to ordain and enact, by the assent of your Lords spiritual and temporal and the Commons in this your present Parliament assembled, and by authority of the same, that no person or persons of this your realm, or of any other your dominions, shall from henceforth pay any pensions, censes, portions, Peter's Pence or any other impositions, to the use of the said Bishop, or of the see of Rome, . . . but that all such pensions, censes, portions and Peter's Pence, . . . shall from henceforth clearly surcease, and never more be levied, taken, perceived, nor paid to any person or persons in any manner of wise. . . .

II   And be it further enacted . . . that neither your Highness, your heirs nor successors, kings of this realm, nor any your subjects of this realm, nor of any other your dominions, shall from henceforth sue to the said Bishop of Rome, called the Pope, or to the see of Rome, or to any persons having or pretending any authority by the same, for licences, dispensations . . . or any other instruments or writings, of what kind, name, nature or quality soever they be of, for any cause or matter, for the which any licence [etc.] . . . heretofore hath been . . . obtained at the see of Rome. . . .

But that from henceforth every such licence [etc.] . . . necessary for your Highness, your heirs or successors, and your and their people and subjects . . . shall be granted, had, and obtained . . . within this your realm, and other your dominions, and not elsewhere, in manner and form following, and none otherwise; that is to say: the Archbishop of Canterbury for the time being, and his successors, shall have power and authority, from time to time, by their discretions, to give, grant, and dispose, by an instrument under the seal of the said Archbishop, unto your Majesty, and to your heirs and successors, kings of this realm, as well all manner such licences [etc.] . . . for causes not being contrary or repugnant to the Holy Scriptures and laws of God, as heretofore hath been used and accustomed to be had and obtained . . . at the see of Rome . . . and all other licences, [etc.] . . . upon all such causes and matters as shall be convenient and necessary to be had, for the honour and surety of your Highness, your heirs and successors and the wealth and profit of this your realm; so that the said Archbishop or any his successors in no manner wise shall grant any dispensation . . . or any other writing . . . for any cause or matter repugnant to the law of Almighty God.

* * *

[IV-VII Any dispensation costing £4 or more is to be confirmed by the King before it is 'put in execution'; the fees to be charged henceforth for the various kinds of dispensation – these fees cover the cost of 'the parchment, wax and silk' and the writing, sealing, enrolling, etc. – are to be at a fixed rate and made public.

* * *

XI If the Archbishop of Canterbury should withhold a dispensation without showing a 'just and reasonable' cause, then the dispensation may be granted by order of the King.]

* * *

XIII Provided always, that this Act, nor any thing or things therein contained, shall be hereafter interpreted or expounded, that your Grace, your nobles and subjects, intend, by the same, to decline or vary from the congregation of Christ's Church in any things concerning the very articles of the Catholic faith of Christendom, or in any other things declared, by Holy Scripture and the word of God, necessary for your and their salvations, but only to make an ordinance by policies necessary and convenient to repress vice, and for good conservation of this realm in peace, unity and tranquillity, from ravin and spoil, ensuing much the old ancient customs of this realm in that behalf; not minding to seek for any reliefs, succours, or remedies for any worldly things and human laws, in any cause of necessity, but, within this realm, at the hands of your Highness, your heirs and successors, kings of this realm, which have and ought to have an imperial power and authority in the same, and not obliged, in any worldly causes, to any other superior.

XIV   Provided alway, that the said Archbishop of Canterbury, or any other person or persons, shall have no power or authority by reason of this Act, to visit or vex any monasteries, abbeys, priories, colleges, hospitals, houses or other places religious, which be or were exempt before the making of this Act, anything in this Act to the contrary thereof notwithstanding; but that redress, visitation, and confirmation shall be had by the King's Highness, his heirs and successors, by commission under the great seal, to be directed to such persons as shall be appointed requisite for the same, in such monasteries, colleges, hospitals, priories, houses and places religious exempt; so that no visitation nor confirmation shall from henceforth be had nor made, in or at any such monasteries [etc.] . . . exempt, by the said Bishop of Rome, nor by any of his authority, nor by any out of the King's dominions; nor that any person, religious or other, resident in any the King's dominions, shall from henceforth depart out of the King's dominions to or for any visitation, congregation or assembly for religion, but that all such visitations, congregations and assemblies shall be within the King's dominions.

*   *   *

[XVI   Any person suing to Rome for any licence, etc., or obeying any censure or other process from Rome, shall incur the penalty of *Praemunire**.

XXI   The King shall have 'power and authority . . . for the ordering, redress and reformation of all manner of indulgences and privileges' within any of the King's dominions previously obtained at Rome.]

*   *   *

Stat. Realm, iii.464-71

8   The Act of Supremacy, 1534 (26 Hen. VIII, c. 1)

It should be noted that as Supreme Head of the Church Henry VIII and his successors exercised *potestas iurisdictionis*, the power to subject the 'spiritualty' to all the laws of the realm, to lay down doctrine, to ensure that such doctrine was adequately taught and to reform the Church in any way they thought necessary. It was never questioned that only the ordained clergy had *potestas ordinis*, the right to preach, to administer the sacraments, absolve, excommunicate, etc. See also 7 above.

Albeit the King's Majesty justly and rightfully is and oweth to be the Supreme Head of the Church of England, and so is recognised by the clergy of this realm in their Convocations, yet nevertheless for corroboration and confirmation thereof, and for increase of virtue in Christ's religion within this realm of England, and to repress and extirp all errors, heresies, and other enormities and abuses heretofore used in the same; be it enacted by authority of this present Parliament, that the King our Sovereign Lord, his heirs and successors, kings of this realm, shall be taken, accepted, and reputed the only Supreme Head in earth of the Church of England, called *Anglicana Ecclesia*, and shall have and enjoy, annexed and united to the imperial Crown of this realm, as well the title and style thereof, as all honours, dignities, pre-eminences, jurisdictions, privileges, authorities, immunities, profits, and commodities, to the said dignity of Supreme Head of the same Church belonging and appertaining; and that our said Sovereign Lord, his heirs and successors, kings of this realm, shall have full power and authority from time to time to visit, repress, redress, reform, order, correct, restrain, and amend all such errors, heresies, abuses, offences, contempts, and enormities, whatsoever they be, which by any manner spiritual authority or jurisdiction ought or may lawfully be reformed, repressed, ordered, redressed, corrected, restrained, or amended, most to the pleasure of Almighty God, the increase of virtue in Christ's religion, and for the conservation of the peace, unity and tranquillity of this realm; any usage, custom, foreign laws, foreign authority, prescription, or any other thing or things to the contrary hereof notwithstanding.

Stat. Realm, iii.492

9 Act annexing First fruits* and Tenths to the Crown, 1534 (26 Hen. VIII, c. 3)

The Act in Conditional Restraint of Annates* (4 above) had condemned these payments to Rome as 'intolerable' exactions. Nevertheless, not only are the entire 'first fruits, revenues and profits for one year' on new benefices now annexed to the Crown, but they become payable by all those entering any new living or ecclesiastical office, secular or monastic, from the highest to the lowest in the Church. In addition, under § VIII, tenths become payable to the Crown annually. This Act therefore greatly increased the financial burdens of the English clergy: in such circumstances the preamble can only be regarded as a masterpiece of drafting. An Act in the following year exempted the clergy from paying tenths during their first year, for which they paid first fruits, and another exempted Oxford and Cambridge, and Eton and Winchester, from both charges. Mary renounced this form of ecclesiastical revenue but in 1559 Elizabeth resumed it, exempting rectories not exceeding 10 marks (£6 13s. 4d.) per annum and vicarages not exceeding £10 per annum.

The commissions provided for in § IX resulted in the *Valor Ecclesiasticus* (see **V, 1**).

In 1540 a special Court was set up for the purpose of collecting first fruits and tenths. Between 1535 and 1547 the Church seems to have paid about £47,000 annually to the King in first fruits, tenths and clerical subsidies.

Forasmuch as it is and of very duty ought to be the natural inclination of all good people, like most faithful, loving and obedient subjects, sincerely and willingly to desire to provide not only for the public weal of their native country but also for the supportation, maintenance and defence of the royal estate of their most dread, benign and gracious Sovereign Lord, upon whom and in whom dependeth all their joy and wealth [here means welfare], in whom also is united and knit so princely a heart and courage, mixed with mercy, wisdom and justice, and also a natural affection joined to the same, as by the great, inestimable and benevolent arguments thereof being most bountifully, largely and many times showed, ministered and approved towards his loving and obedient subjects hath well appeared, which requireth a like correspondence of gratitude to be considered according to their most bounden duties; wherefore his said humble and obedient subjects, as well the Lords spiritual and temporal as the Commons in this present Parliament assembled, calling to their remembrance not only the manifold and innumerable benefits daily administered by his Highness to them all, and to the residue of all other his subjects of this realm, but also how long time his Majesty hath most victoriously by his high wisdom and policy protected, defended and governed this his realm and maintained his people and subjects of the same in tranquillity, peace, unity, quietness and wealth; and also considering what great, excessive and inestimable charges his Highness hath heretofore been at and sustained by the space of five and twenty whole years, and also daily sustaineth for the maintenance, tuition and defence of this his realm and his loving subjects of the same, which cannot be sustained and borne without some honourable provision and remedy may be found, provided and ordained for maintenance thereof, do therefore desire and most humbly pray that for the more surety of continuance and augmentation of his Highness's royal estate, being not only now recognised (as he always in deed heretofore hath been) the only Supreme Head in earth next and immediately under God of the Church of England, but also their most assured and undoubted natural Sovereign liege Lord and King, having the whole governance, tuition, defence and maintenance of this his realm and most loving, obedient subjects of the same:

It may therefore be ordained and enacted . . . that the King's Highness, his heirs and successors . . . shall have and enjoy from time to time, to endure for ever, of every such person . . . which at any time after the first day of January next coming shall be nominated, elected . . . presented, collated, or by any other means appointed to have any archbishopric, bishopric, abbacy, monastery, priory, college, hospital, archdeaconry, deanery, provostship, prebend, parsonage, vicarage, chantry,* free chapel, or other dignity, benefice, office or promotion spiritual within this realm or elsewhere within any of the King's dominions, of what name, nature or quality soever they be or to whose foundation, patronage or gift soever they belong, the first fruits, revenues and profits for one year of every such archbishopric, bishopric [and all benefices and ecclesiastical offices mentioned above] . . . and that every such person . . . before any actual or real possession or meddling with the profits of any such archbishopric, bishopric [etc.] . . . shall satisfy, content and pay, or compound or agree to pay to the King's use at reasonable days upon good sureties the said first fruits and profits for one year.

*   *   *

VIII   And over this be it enacted . . . that the King's Majesty, his heirs and successors . . . for more augmentation and maintenance of the royal estate of his imperial Crown and dignity of Supreme Head of the Church of England, shall yearly have, take [and] enjoy . . . one yearly rent or pension amounting to the value of the tenth part of all the revenues, farms [fixed annual rents], tithes*, offerings, emoluments and of all other profits, as well called spiritual as temporal, now appertaining or belonging or that hereafter shall belong to any archbishopric, bishopric [etc. as above] . . . within any diocese of this realm or in Wales; the said pension or annual rent to be yearly paid for ever to our said Sovereign Lord. [To begin at Christmas, 1535.]

[IX Commissions shall be appointed 'to examine, search and enquire
... of and for the true and just whole and entire yearly values of all
the manors, lands [and other property] ... belonging to any archbishopric, bishopric' [etc.]]

*   *   *

Stat. Realm, iii.493-9

10   Bishop Stephen Gardiner on 'True Obedience,' 1535

Stephen Gardiner (c. 1490-1555), a doctor of civil and canon law, became Bishop
of Winchester in 1531 and was also Master of Trinity Hall, Cambridge (1525-49).
He served as ambassador to the French court in 1531-2 and was employed in
various diplomatic negotiations, including those concerning the royal divorce.
Under Edward VI his opposition to Reformation doctrines led to his imprisonment and deprivation. Restored to his see by Mary, he was Lord Chancellor
until his death in 1555.
De Vera Obedientia was published in London by the King's printer Berthelet
immediately after its composition in 1535. Editions were also quickly published
in Strassburg and Hamburg. Edmund Bonner, who became Bishop of London
in 1539, and was to prove as uncompromising as Gardiner in defending traditional doctrines, wrote a violently anti-papal preface to the Hamburg edition.
The treatise was translated into English in 1553, probably by the Protestant
John Bale. In spite of some misconstructions, the translation accurately conveys
the sense of the original in the following extracts. In the same year in which
Gardiner wrote in support of the Royal Supremacy, Sir Thomas More repudi-
ated it with equal firmness: 11 below.

[Throughout his treatise Gardiner stresses the overwhelming importance of obedience to God and to his word, Christ being the supreme
exemplar of this obedience. There is in societies a natural hierarchy of
command: wives obey their husbands, servants their masters; all obey
their prince, whom God has put in authority over them and who in
his person 'representeth as it were the image of God upon earth'. Thus,
in obeying the prince, we obey God and this is 'true obedience'. The
Bishop of Rome has spiritual authority only over those in his own
diocese and it is now clear that the Scriptures gave him no 'supremacy
of worldly administration'. Christ is of course the Head of the Church,

but the prince is 'the Supreme Head in earth'. Gardiner quotes many
biblical texts to support his contentions.]

I think it requisite for me ... to touch also in this place that cause
which is ... spoken of at this day almost in all men's hands and in all
men's mouths: whether the whole consent of Englishmen be grounded
upon God's law in that they declare and honour the most victorious
and most noble prince Henry VIII King of England and of France,
defender of the faith and Lord of Ireland, to be in earth the Supreme
Head of the Church of England, and is granted unto him by authority
thereof in the open Court of Parliament freely to use his right and to
call himself Supreme Head of the Church of England as well in name
as in deed. Wherein there is no newly invented matter wrought, only
their will was to have the power pertaining to a prince by God's law
to be the more clearly expressed with a more fit term to express it by,
namely, for this purpose to withdraw that counterfeit vain opinion out
of the common people's minds which the false pretensed power of the
Bishop of Rome had for the space of certain years blinded them withall,
to the great impeachment of the King's authority, which all men are
bounden to wish and to their uttermost power see kept safe, restored,
and defended from wrongs. Wherein surely I see no cause why any
man should be offended that the King is called the Head of [the] Church
of England rather than the Head of the realm of England ... the
Church of England consisteth of the same sorts of people at this day
that are comprised in this word realm of whom the King is called the
Head. Shall he not, being called the Head of the realm of England, be
also the Head of the same men when they are named the Church of
England? ... What a folly were it then for a man to confess that all
one man ... dwelling in England is in subjection to the King as unto
the Head: and if ye call him a Christian of the same sort to say that he
is not a subject? ... (Sig. C viii b – Sig. D ii a)

[Gardiner now refers to famous New Testament texts on the necessity
for obedience to the temporal power.] But here some men will say to
me: you travail about that that no man is in doubt of. For who ever
denied that the prince ought to be obeyed? ... For it is certain that
obedience is due, but how far the limits of requiring obedience extend:
that is all the whole question that can be demanded. What manner of
limits are those that ye tell me of, seeing the Scripture hath none such?
... [Some men think] that the prince should govern in temporal matters and the church in spiritual: after the which distinction the prince,

as the moon which is called the less light, should have charge of such matters as are of the night, but the other which be of the spirit and of the daylight he must reserve to the sun alone to be discussed. Forsooth a blind distinction and full of darkness. . . . (Sig. D iiii a – Sig. D vi b)

. . . there is not found in the holy Scriptures so much as one syllable of the Bishop of Rome. . . . [There] is no mention made of Peter's Supremacy. . . . I flee to the interpretation of the word that it may agree with the right proper meaning of the gospel expressed in Christ's deeds. Admit that Peter were chief, admit he had the Supremacy of Christ, what of that? Was a kingdom, lordship or pre-eminence given him with the Supremacy? Because he was bidden to confirm his brethren in faith was it given him to bear rule over his brethren therefore? Christ's humble estate knew no such kind of speech nor matter. . . . (Sig. F iii a – Sig. F iiii a)

All sorts of people are agreed . . . with most steadfast consent, learned and unlearned, both men and women: that no manner of person born and brought up in England hath ought to do with Rome. All manner of people receiving and embracing the truth do with one whole consent acknowledge, honour, and reverence the King for the Supreme Head of the Church upon earth. They bid the Bishop of Rome farewell . . . yet all men for Christian charity's sake pray for him and wish him well, among whom I am one specially: . . . (Sig. G iiii a – Sig. iiii b)

Let us then follow the order that God hath prescribed . . . let us follow the truth itself: let us obey it, let us do after it which only maketh true obedience. (Sig. G v b – Sig. G vi a)

Stephen Gardiner, *De Vera Obedientia* (Nov., 1553 edition)

11 Thomas More discharges his Conscience

In the reign of Mary, Nicholas Harpsfield wrote the first formal biography of More; he used many earlier sources, including the life by More's son-in-law, William Roper. The text of Harpsfield has been prepared from the numerous surviving manuscripts and published by the Early English Text Society. As an appendix to this edition is printed the contemporary Paris News Letter, which formed Harpsfield's main source for the following passages. In making his final speech, after the verdict had gone against him, More may not have used these precise words, but they admirably express the convictions which led him to embrace martyrdom. He was executed on 6 July 1535.

'Seeing that I see ye are determined to condemn me (God knoweth how) I will now in discharge of my conscience speak my mind plainly and freely, touching my indictment and your Statute withall. And forasmuch as this indictment is grounded upon an Act of Parliament directly repugnant to the laws of God and his holy Church, the supreme government of which, or of any part whereof, may no temporal prince presume by any law to take upon him, as rightfully belonging to the see of Rome, a spiritual pre-eminence by the mouth of our Saviour himself, personally present upon earth, only to St. Peter and his successors, bishops of the same see, by special prerogative granted; it is therefore in law amongst Christian men, insufficient to charge any Christian man.'

And for proof thereof, like as among divers other reasons and authorities he declared that this realm, being but one member and small part of the Church, might not make a particular law disagreeable with the general law of Christ's universal Catholic Church, no more than the city of London, being but one poor member in respect of the whole realm, might make a law against an Act of Parliament to bind the whole realm. So further showed he that it was contrary both to the laws and statutes of our own land yet unrepealed, as they might evidently perceive in Magna Carta (*Quod ecclesia Anglicana libera sit, et habeat omnia iura sua integra, et libertates suas illaesas* [That the English Church shall be free, and shall have its rights undiminished and its liberties unimpaired]); and also contrary to the sacred oath which the King's Highness himself and every Christian prince always with great solemnity received at their coronations, alleging moreover that no more might this realm of England refuse obedience to the see of Rome than might the child refuse obedience to his own natural father. . . .

Then was it by the Lord Chancellor thereunto answered that seeing all the bishops, universities and best learned men of the realm had to this Act agreed, it was much marvel that he alone against them all would so stiffly stick thereat, and so vehemently argue thereagainst. . . .

To this Sir Thomas More replied, saying that these seven years seriously and earnestly he had beset his studies and cogitations upon this point chiefly, among other, of the pope's authority. 'Neither as yet', said he, 'have I chanced upon any ancient writer or doctor that so advanceth, as your Statute doth, the supremacy of any secular and temporal prince. If there were no more but myself upon my side, and the whole Parliament upon the other, I would be sore afraid to lean to mine own mind only against so many. But if the number of bishops and universities be so material as your lordship seemeth to take it, then see I little cause, my lord, why that thing in my conscience should make any change. For I nothing doubt but that, though not in this realm, yet in Christendom about, of these well-learned bishops and virtuous men that are still alive, they be not the fewer part that are of my mind therein. But if I should speak of those that are already dead, of whom many be now holy saints in heaven, I am very sure it is the far greater part of them that, all the while they lived, thought in this case that way that I think now; and therefore am I not bounden, my lord, to conform my conscience to the Council of one realm against the general Council of Christendom. For of the foresaid holy bishops I have, for every bishop of yours, above one hundred. And for one Council or Parliament of yours (God knoweth what manner of one), I have all the Councils made these thousand years. And for this one Kingdom, I have all other Christian realms.'

Nicholas Harpsfield, *The life and death of Sir Thomas More*, ed. E. V. Hitchcock and R. W. Chambers (*Early English Text Society*, original series, clxxxvi, 1932), pp. 193-6

IV

MATTERS OF DOCTRINE AND DISCIPLINE, 1536-8

1 Proclamation Restricting the Number of Holy-days, 1536

This decree, made in Convocation and confirmed by the King's authority, was issued in the summer of 1536, shortly before the First Royal Injunctions (3 below). It was amended by 5 & 6 Edw. VI, c. 3, whereby all Sundays and 25 other specified days should be kept as holy-days, though all persons could work on these days in harvest-time, or at other times 'when necessity shall require'. This latter Act was repealed by Mary. Under Elizabeth the Calendar before the Book of Common Prayer directed which holy-days should be observed.

Forasmuch as the number of holy-days is so excessively grown, and yet daily more and more by men's devotion, yea rather superstition, was like further to increase, that the same was . . . not only prejudicial to the common weal, by reason that it is occasion as well of much sloth and idleness, the very nurse of thieves, vagabonds, and of divers other unthriftiness and inconveniences, as of decay of good mysteries [crafts] and arts profitable and necessary for the commonwealth, and loss of man's food (many times being clean destroyed through the superstitious observance of the said holy-days, in not taking the opportunity of good and serene weather offered upon the same in time of harvest), but also pernicious to the souls of many men, who, being enticed by the licentious vacation and liberty of those holy-days, do upon the same commonly use and practise more excess, riot and superfluity, than upon any other days. And since the Sabbath-day was used and ordained but for man's use, and therefore ought to give place to the necessity and behoof of the same, whensoever that shall occur, much rather than any other holy-day instituted by man: it is therefore by the King's Highness's authority as Supreme Head in earth of the Church of England, with the common assent and consent of the prelates and clergy of this his realm, in Convocation lawfully assembled and congregated, amongst other things decreed, ordained and established:

[Detailed instructions are then given regarding the reduced number of holy-days to be observed in future. There are to be no holy-days observed either in harvest time (to count from 1 July to 29 September), or during the law-terms at Westminster, except on a few days e.g. Ascension Day, when the judges did not sit. On days no longer to be observed as holy-days 'it shall be lawful to all and singular persons . . . to go to their work', but the holy-days prescribed are to be kept 'holy and solemnly of every man'.]

Foxe, v.164-5

2   The Ten Articles, 1536

These Articles, the first of the Henrician formularies of the Faith, were adopted by Convocation at the wish of the King and were imposed by his sole authority. They have often been interpreted as conciliatory to the German Lutherans, with whom political negotiations were currently being conducted. Undoubtedly some of the phraseology and general approach (as in Article V) show a degree of Lutheran influence, even whilst avoiding any definite commitment. At the same time, the orthodox doctrinal views of the King and the conservative group are represented, e.g. in the retention of auricular confession in penance, which itself is described as a sacrament of divine institution. Article IV admits of either a Lutheran interpretation of the eucharist or of transubstantiation*. It will be noted that of the seven traditional sacraments only three are expounded – those of baptism, penance and the altar. These are regarded as 'necessary to our salvation', a point re-emphasised in item II of the First Royal Injunctions (3 below). The first signature appended to the Articles, heading those of prelates and other divines, was that of Thomas Cromwell, whom the King had made his vicegerent, thus investing him with power to execute all the functions which the King claimed as Supreme Head of the English Church.

[Preface: The King stresses his duty to ensure 'unity and concord in opinion'. Unfortunately diversity in opinions has lately grown. Therefore the following Articles have been devised 'after long and mature deliberation' and are issued in order 'to eschew not only the dangers of souls, but also the outward unquietness which by occasion of the said diversity in opinions (if remedy were not provided) might perchance have ensued'. For better understanding, the King has caused 'the said Articles to be divided into two sorts': I-V are those which 'be necessary to our salvation'; VI-X concern 'such things as have been of a long continuance for a decent order and honest policy . . . although they be not expressly commanded of God, nor necessary to our salvation'.

Article I emphasises the necessity for the clergy to teach and the people to believe all those things 'which be comprehended in the whole body and canon of the Bible' and also in the three Creeds in common liturgical use.

Article II, after defining the sacrament of baptism in an orthodox sense' ends with the words 'according also to the saying of St. Paul . . . God hath not saved us for the works of justice which we have done, but of his mercy by baptism, and renovation of the Holy Ghost . . .'.]

III The sacrament of penance . . . was institute of Christ in the New Testament as a thing so necessary for man's salvation, that no man which after his baptism is fallen again, and hath committed deadly sin can without the same be saved or attain everlasting life. . . . [The order necessarily to be followed is then set out: contrition, auricular confession and absolution, and thirdly the penance itself.] . . . By penance and . . . good works of [charity] . . . we shall not only obtain everlasting life, but also we shall deserve remission or mitigation of these present pains and afflictions in this world. . . .

IV As touching the sacrament of the altar . . . our people . . . must constantly believe that under the form and figure of bread and wine, which we there presently do see and perceive by outward senses, is verily, substantially and really contained and comprehended the very selfsame body and blood of our Saviour Jesus Christ . . . [which] is corporally, really and in the very substance exhibited, distributed and received . . . of all them which receive the said sacrament, and that therefore the said sacrament is to be used with all due reverence and honour, and that every man ought first to prove and examine himself, and religiously to try and search his own conscience, before he shall receive the same. . . . For whosoever eateth it or drinketh it unworthily, he eateth and drinketh it to his own damnation; because he putteth no difference between the very body of Christ and other kinds of meat.

V   Fifthly, as touching the order and cause of our justification . . . sinners attain this justification by contrition and faith joined with charity, after such sort . . . as we before mentioned [in III above] . . . not as though our contrition, or faith, or any works proceeding thereof, can worthily merit or deserve to attain the said justification; for the only mercy and grace of the Father, promised freely unto us for his Son's sake, Jesus Christ, and the merits of his blood and passion, be the only sufficient and worthy causes thereof: and yet that notwithstanding, to the attaining of the same justification, God requireth to be in us not only inward contrition, perfect faith and charity, certain hope and confidence, with all other spiritual graces and motions, which . . . must necessarily concur in . . . our justification; but also he requireth and commandeth us, that after we be justified we must also have good works of charity and obedience toward God, in the observing and fulfilling outwardly of his laws and commandments. . . .

VI   As touching images . . . especially the images of Christ and Our Lady . . . it is meet that they should stand in the churches. . . . As for kneeling and offering unto them . . . the people ought to be diligently taught that they in no wise do it, nor think it meet to be done to the same images, but only to be done to God, and in his honour, although it be done before the images. . . .

[VII   'As touching the honouring of saints', they should be reverenced 'for their excellent virtues which [Christ] planted in them' but 'not with that confidence and honour which are only due unto God'.]

VIII   As touching praying to saints . . . albeit grace, remission of sin, and salvation, cannot be obtained but of God only by the mediation of our Saviour Christ, which is only sufficient mediator for our sins, yet it is very laudable to pray to saints in heaven everlastingly living, whose charity is ever permanent, to be intercessors . . . so that it be done without any vain superstition, as to think that any saint is more merciful, or will hear us sooner than Christ. . . .

IX   As concerning the rites and ceremonies of Christ's Church [the sprinkling of holy water, bearing of candles on Candlemas-day etc., these are 'not to be contemned and cast away'] but to be used and continued as things good and laudable. . . . But none of these ceremonies have power to remit sin, but only to stir and lift up our minds unto God, by whom only our sins be forgiven.

X [of Purgatory*] . . . it is a very good and a charitable deed to pray for souls departed . . . no man ought to be grieved with the continuance of the same . . . : but forasmuch as the place where they be, the name thereof, and kind of pains there, also be to us uncertain by Scripture; therefore this with all other things we remit to Almighty God. . . . Wherefore it is much necessary that such abuses be clearly put away, which under the name of purgatory hath been advanced, as to make men believe that through the Bishop of Rome's pardons souls might clearly be delivered out of purgatory and all the pains of it, or that masses said . . . might likewise deliver them from all their pain, and send them straight to heaven; and other like abuses.

Charles Hardwick, A History of the Articles of Religion (1890), Appendix I, pp. 237-58

3   The First Royal Injunctions of Henry VIII, 1536

The two sets of Injunctions (1536, 1538) were drawn up by Cromwell in his capacity as vicegerent. The importance of their social and educational implications is emphasised in the **Introduction**, pp. 7-8. The attack made in the First Injunctions on what were considered to be idolatrous or superstitious practices was carried a good deal further in the Second (4 below).

In the name of God, Amen. In the year of our Lord God 1536, and of the most noble reign of our Sovereign Lord Henry VIII, King of England and of France . . . I, Thomas Cromwell, knight, Lord Cromwell, Keeper of the Privy Seal of our said Sovereign Lord the King, and vicegerent unto the same, for and concerning all his jurisdiction ecclesiastical within this realm, visiting by the King's Highness's Supreme authority ecclesiastical the people and clergy of this deanery of ———— by my trusty commissary ———— lawfully deputed and constituted for this part, have to the glory of Almighty God, to the King's Highness's honour, the public weal of this his realm, and increase of virtue in the same, appointed and assigned these Injunctions ensuing, to be kept and observed of the dean, parsons, vicars, curates, and stipendiaries resident or having cure of souls, or any other spiritual administration within this deanery, under the pains hereafter limited and appointed.

I The first is, that the dean, parsons, vicars, and others having cure of souls anywhere within this deanery, shall faithfully keep and observe, and as far as in them may lie, shall cause to be observed and kept of other, all and singular laws and statutes of this realm made for the abolishing and extirpation of the Bishop of Rome's pretensed and usurped power and jurisdiction within this realm, and for the establishment and confirmation of the King's authority and jurisdiction within the same, as of the Supreme Head of the Church of England, and shall to the uttermost of their wit, knowledge and learning, purely, sincerely, and without any colour or dissimulation declare, manifest, and open for the space of one quarter of a year now next ensuing, once every Sunday, and after that at the leastwise twice every quarter, in their sermons and other collations, that the Bishop of Rome's usurped power and jurisdiction, having no establishment nor ground by the law of God, was of most just causes taken away and abolished; and therefore they owe unto him no manner of obedience or subjection, and that the King's power is within his dominion the highest power and potentate under God, to whom all men within the same dominion by God's commandment owe most loyalty and obedience, afore and above all other powers and potentates in earth.

II Item, whereas certain Articles [The 10 Articles: 2 above] were lately devised and put forth by the King's Highness's authority, and condescended upon [agreed] by the prelates and clergy of this his realm, in Convocation, whereof part are necessary to be holden and believed for our salvation, and the other part do concern and touch certain laudable ceremonies, rites, and usages of the Church meet and convenient to be kept and used for a decent and a politic order in the same; the said dean, parsons, vicars, and other curates shall so open and declare in their said sermons and other collations the said Articles unto them that be under their cure, that they may plainly know and discern which of them be necessary to be believed and observed for their salvation; and which be not necessary, but only do concern the decent and politic order of the said Church, according to such commandment and admonition as has been given to them heretofore by authority of the King's Highness in that behalf.

[III orders that the reduced number of holy-days, specified in the recent proclamation, shall be observed with propriety: (1 above).]

IV   Besides this, to the intent that all superstition and hypocrisy, crept into divers men's hearts, may vanish away, they shall not set forth or extol any images, relics, or miracles for any superstition or lucre, nor allure the people by any enticements to the pilgrimage of any saint, otherwise than is permitted in the Articles lately put forth . . . as though it were proper or peculiar to that saint to give this commodity or that, seeing all goodness, health, and grace ought to be both asked and looked for only of God, as of the very author of the same, and of none other, for without him that cannot be given; but they shall exhort as well their parishioners as other pilgrims, that they do rather apply themselves to the keeping of God's commandments and fulfilling of his works of charity, persuading them that they shall please God more by the true exercising of their bodily labour, travail, or occupation, and providing for their families, than if they went about to the said pilgrimages; and that it shall profit more their soul's health, if they do bestow that on the poor and needy, which they would have bestowed upon the said images or relics.

V   Also in the same their sermons and other collations, the parsons, vicars, and other curates abovesaid shall diligently admonish the fathers and mothers, masters and governors of youth, being within their cure, to teach or cause to be taught their children and servants, even from their infancy, their 'Paternoster', the Articles of our faith [the Creed], and the Ten Commandments in their mother tongue; and the same so taught, shall cause the said youth oft to repeat and understand; and to the intent this may be the more easily done, the said curates shall in their sermons deliberately and plainly recite oft the said 'Paternoster', the Articles of our faith, and the Ten Commandments, one clause or Article one day, and another another day, till the whole be taught and learned by little; and shall deliver the same in writing, or show where printed books containing the same are to be sold, to them that can read or will desire the same; and thereto that the said fathers and mothers, masters and governors do bestow their children and servants, even from their childhood, either to learning, or to some other honest exercise, occupation, or husbandry, exhorting, counselling, and by all the ways and means they may, as well in their said sermons and collations, as other ways, persuading the said fathers, mothers, masters, and other governors, being under their cure and charge, diligently to provide and foresee that the said youth be in no manner wise kept or brought up in idleness, lest at any time afterward they be driven, for lack of some mystery [craft] or occupation to live by, to fall to begging, stealing or some other unthriftiness; forasmuch as we may daily see through sloth and idleness divers valiant men fall, some to begging and some to theft and murder, which after, brought to calamity and misery, imputed great part thereof to their friends and governors, which suffered them to be brought up so idly in their youth; where if they had been well educated and brought up in some good literature, occupation, or mystery, they should, being rulers of their own family, have profited as well themselves, as divers other persons, to the great commodity and ornament of the common weal.

VI   Also, that the said parsons, vicars, and other curates shall diligently provide that sacraments and sacramentals be duly and reverently ministered in their parishes; and if at any time it happen them other [than] in any of the cases expressed in the statutes of this realm, or of special licence given by the King's Majesty, to be absent from their benefices, they shall leave their cures, not to a rude and unlearned person, but to an honest, well learned, and expert curate, that may teach the rude and unlearned of their cure wholesome doctrine, and reduce them to the right way that do err; and always let them see that neither they nor their vicars do seek more their own profit, promotion, or advantage, than the profit of the souls that they have under their cure, or the glory of God.

VII   Also, the said dean, parsons, vicars, curates, and other priests shall in no wise, at any unlawful time, nor for any other cause than for their honest necessity, haunt or resort to any taverns or alehouses, and after their dinner or supper they shall not give themselves to drinking or riot, spending their time idly, by day or by night, at tables or card-playing, or any other unlawful game; but at such times as they shall have such leisure they shall read or hear somewhat of holy Scripture, or shall occupy themselves with some other honest exercise, and that they always do those things which appertain to good congruence and honesty, with profit of the commonweal, having always in mind that they ought to excel all other in purity of life, and should be example to all other to live well and Christianly.

VIII   Furthermore, because the goods of the Church are called the goods of the poor, and at these days nothing is less seen than the poor to be sustained with the same, all parsons, vicars, pensionaries, prebendaries, and other beneficed men within this deanery, not being resident upon their benefices, which may dispend yearly twenty pounds _said_

or above within this deanery or elsewhere, shall distribute hereafter yearly amongst their poor parishioners, or other inhabitants there, in the presence of the churchwardens or some other honest men of the parish, the fortieth part of the fruits and revenues of their said benefices, lest they be worthily noted of ingratitude, which, reserving so many parts to themselves, cannot vouchsafe to impart the fortieth portion thereof amongst the poor people of that parish, that is so fruitful and profitable unto them.

IX   And to the intent that learned men may hereafter spring the more for the execution of the premises, every parson, vicar, clerk, or beneficed man within this deanery, having yearly to dispend, in benefices and other promotions of the Church, an hundred pounds, shall give competent exhibition to one scholar, and for as many hundred pounds more as he may dispend, to so many scholars more shall give like exhibition in the University of Oxford or Cambridge, or some grammar school, which, after they have profited in good learning, may be partners of their patron's cure and charge, as well in preaching as otherwise in the execution of their offices, or may, when need shall be, otherwise profit the commonwealth with their counsel and wisdom.

X   Also, that all parsons, vicars, and clerks, having churches, chapels, or mansions within this deanery, shall bestow yearly hereafter upon the same mansions or chancels of their churches, being in decay, the fifth part of their benefices, till they be fully repaired, and the same, so repaired, shall always keep and maintain in good state.

All which and singular Injunctions shall be inviolably observed of the said dean, parsons, vicars, curates, stipendiaries, and other clerks and beneficed men, under the pain of suspension and sequestration of the fruits of their benefices, until they have done their duty according to these Injunctions.

Gee and Hardy, pp. 269-74, from Cranmer's Register, fo. 97b

4   The Second Royal Injunctions of Henry VIII, 1538

Of great importance in the Second Injunctions are items II and XII. Further details about the English Bible are given in **VI, 2**. In regard to item XII, relatively few parish registers of this early period are extant, but many are continuous from the reign of Edward VI and still more from the early years of Elizabeth. The introduction of parish registers forms a major administrative landmark; it had a special importance in view of the complicated laws on kinship and matrimony. See also **3** above.

[The first item instructs all clergy to observe the First Injunctions.]

II Item, that you shall provide on this side the feast of Easter next coming, one book of the whole Bible of the largest volume, in English, and the same set up in some convenient place within the said church that you have cure of, whereas your parishioners may most commodiously resort to the same and read it; the charges of which book shall be rateably borne between you, the parson, and the parishioners aforesaid, that is to say, the one half by you, and the other half by them.

III Item, that you shall discourage no man privily or apertly [secretly or openly] from the reading or hearing of the said Bible, but shall expressly provoke, stir, and exhort every person to read the same, as that which is the very lively word of God, that every Christian man is bound to embrace, believe, and follow, if he look to be saved; admonishing them nevertheless, to avoid all contention and altercation therein, and to use an honest sobriety in the inquisition of the true sense of the same, and refer the explication of obscure places to men of higher judgment in Scripture.

[IV again exhorts the clergy (as in the First Injunctions) to teach the Lord's Prayer, the Creed, and the Ten Commandments, in English, so that they may be gradually learnt by heart.]

V Item, that you shall in confessions every Lent examine every person that comes to confession to you, whether they can recite the Articles of our faith and the 'Paternoster', in English, and hear them say the same; particularly wherein if they be not perfect, you shall declare to the same that every Christian person ought to know the same before they should receive the blessed sacrament of the altar, and monish them to learn the same more perfectly by the next year following, or else like as they ought not to presume to come to God's board without perfect knowledge of the same; and if they do, it is to the great peril of their souls. . . .

VI Item, that you shall make, or cause to be made in the said church, and every other cure you have, one sermon every quarter of the year at the least, wherein you shall purely and sincerely declare the very

gospel of Christ, and in the same exhort your hearers to the works of
charity, mercy, and faith, specially prescribed and commanded in
Scripture, and not to repose their trust or affiance in any other works
devised by men's phantasies beside Scripture; as in wandering to pilgrimages, offering of money, candles, or tapers to images or relics, or
kissing or licking the same, saying over a number of beads, not understood or minded on, or in such-like superstition, for the doing whereof
you not only have no promise of reward in Scripture, but contrariwise,
great threats and maledictions of God, as things tending to idolatry
and superstition, which of all other offences God Almighty does most
detest and abhor, for that the same diminishes most his honour
and glory.

VII   Item, that such feigned images as you know in any of your cures
to be so abused with pilgrimages or offerings of anything made thereunto, you shall for avoiding that most detestable offence of idolatry
forthwith take down and delay, and shall suffer from henceforth no
candles, tapers, or images of wax to be set afore any image or picture,
but only the light that commonly goeth across the church by the rood
loft, the light before the sacrament of the altar, and the light about the
sepulchre, which for the adorning of the church and divine service you
shall suffer to remain; still admonishing your parishioners that images
serve for none other purpose but as to be books of unlearned men that
cannot know letters, whereby they might be otherwise admonished
of the lives and conversation of them that the said images do represent;
which images, if they abuse for any other intent than for such remem-
brances, they commit idolatry in the same to the great danger of their
souls: and therefore the King's Highness, graciously tendering the weal
of his subjects' souls, has in part already, and more will hereafter travail
for the abolishing of such images, as might be occasion of so great an
offence to God, and so great a danger to the souls of his loving subjects.

VIII   Item, that all in such benefices or cures as you have, whereupon
you be not yourself resident, you shall appoint such curates in your
stead, as both can by their ability, and will also promptly execute these
Injunctions and do their duty; otherwise that you are bound in every
behalf accordingly, and may profit their cure no less with good example
of living, than with declaration of the word of God; or else their lack
and defaults shall be imputed unto you, who shall straitly answer for
the same, if they do otherwise.

IX   Item, that you shall admit no man to preach within any your benefices or cures, but such as shall appear unto you to be sufficiently licensed thereunto by the King's Highness or his Grace's authority, by the Archbishop of Canterbury, or the bishop of this diocese; and such as shall be so licensed you shall gladly receive to declare the word of God, without any resistance or contradiction.

X   Item, if you have heretofore declared to your parishioners anything to the extolling or setting forth of pilgrimages, feigned relics, or images, or any such superstition, you shall now openly, afore the same, recant and reprove the same, showing them, as the truth is, that you did the same upon no ground of Scripture, but as one being led and seduced by a common error and abuse crept into the Church, through the sufferance and avarice of such as felt profit by the same.

XI   Item, if you do or shall know any man within your parish, or elsewhere, that is a letter [hinderer] of the word of God to be read in English, or sincerely preached, or of the execution of these Injunctions, or a fautor [abettor] of the Bishop of Rome's pretensed power, now by the law of this realm justly rejected and extirped, you shall detect and present the same to the King's Highness, or his honourable Council, or to his vicegerent aforesaid, or the justice of peace next adjoining.

XII   Item, that you, and every parson, vicar, or curate within this diocese, shall for every church keep one book or register, wherein ye shall write the day and year of every wedding, christening and burying made within your parish for your time, and so every man succeeding you likewise; and also there insert every person's name that shall be so wedded, christened or buried; and for the safe keeping of the same book, the parish shall be bound to provide of their common charges one sure coffer with two locks and keys, whereof the one to remain with you, and the other with the wardens of every such parish, wherein the said book shall be laid up; which book you shall every Sunday take forth, and in the presence of the said wardens, or one of them, write and record in the same all the weddings, christenings and buryings made the whole week before, and that done, to lay up the book in the said coffer as before; and for every time that the same shall be omitted, the party that shall be in the fault thereof shall forfeit to the said church, three shillings and fourpence, to be employed on the reparation of the same church.

XIII   Item, that you shall once every quarter of a year read these and the other former Injunctions given unto you by the authority of the King's Highness, openly and deliberately before all your parishioners, to the intent that both you may be the better admonished of your duty, and your said parishioners the more incited to ensue the same for their part.

XIV   Item, forasmuch as by a law established, every man is bound to pay his tithes*, no man shall, by colour of duty omitted by their curates, detain their tithes, and so redub [redress] one wrong with another, or be his own judge; but shall truly pay the same, as has been accustomed, to their parsons and curates, without any restraint or diminution; and such lack or default as they can justly find in their parsons and curates, to call for reformation thereof at their ordinaries'* and other superiors' hands, who upon complaints and due proof thereof shall reform the same accordingly.

[XV   orders that the clergy are not to alter 'the [prescribed] order and manner of any fasting day' nor of 'any prayer or divine service' without authority. XVI orders the omission of the ringing of the Ave-bell, 'lest the people do hereafter trust to have pardon for the saying their "Aves" between the said knelling, as they have done in times past'.

XVII stresses that it is better to sing those petitions in the Litany which are addressed directly to God rather than those to the saints.]

Gee and Hardy, pp. 275-81, from Cranmer's
Register, fo. 215b

5   Extracts from the Bishops' Book (Institution of a Christian Man), 1537

The *Institution of a Christian Man* was drawn up at the King's command by a large committee of prelates and divines. Thus it came to be called the *Bishops' Book*. After much debate it was completed in July 1537. The King's purpose, as set out by the committee in their preface to Henry, may have been in part inspired by the Pilgrimage of Grace in the autumn of 1536.

Unofficially, the *Bishops' Book* superseded the Ten Articles (2 above), but it was not officially authorised by the King, who merely recommended those with cure of souls to read it. The book shows a greater degree of conservative influence than the Ten Articles; e.g. the four sacraments omitted from the latter are now restored. Nevertheless, these are accorded a lower status than the other three sacraments – those of baptism, of penance, and of the altar, which are expounded as in the Ten Articles, with a few slight alterations in wording. The Articles of Justification and Purgatory* in the Ten Articles are similarly repeated.

The passage concerning the 'holy catholic and universal Church' is perhaps the most significant in the whole work, in that it anticipates so strikingly the future outlook of the Anglican Church.

[In their Preface addressed to the King, the prelates and divines say they have tried to satisfy his command, 'upon the diligent search and perusing of holy Scripture, to set forth a plain and sincere doctrine, concerning the whole sum of all those things which appertain unto the profession of a Christian man, that by the same all errors, doubts, superstitions and abuses might be suppressed, removed and utterly taken away, to the honour of Almighty God, and to the perfect establishing of your said subjects in good unity and concord, and perfect quietness both in their souls and bodies'.

The book takes the form of detailed expositions of (I) the Articles of the Apostles' Creed, (II) the Seven Sacraments, (III) the Ten Commandments, and (IV) the Paternoster and Ave. Extracts are given under these numbered heads.]

(I) ... *The sense and interpretation of the ninth article* ['And I believe that there is one holy catholic and universal Church']. I believe ... that there is and hath been ever from the beginning of the world, and so shall endure and continue for ever, one certain number, society, communion, or company of the elect and faithful people of God; of which number our Saviour Jesu Christ is the only head and governor, and the members of the same be all those holy saints which be now in heaven, and also all the faithful people of God which be now on life, or that ever heretofore have lived, or shall live here in this world. ... [Later it is stated that in addition 'an infinite number of the evil and wicked people' will always have to count as members of this congregation 'here in this world' (provided they have not been excommunicated), not because 'they be such members in very deed' but because until the Last Judgment it will not be known 'who be the very true members of [Christ's] body, and who be not'.]

And I believe assuredly that this Congregation ... is in very deed ... the holy catholic Church. ... And like as citizens assembled in one city do live there under common laws, and in common society, and there do consult, study and labour, each man in his room and office, and according unto his calling, for their common wealth [welfare], and finally be made participant or partakers of all and singular such benefits and commodities as do arise unto them thereby; even so I believe that the members of this holy catholic Church or Congregation be collected and gathered together within the same Church as within one city or fold, and that they be therein all united and incorporated by the holy spirit of Christ into one body, and that they do live there all in one faith, one hope, one charity, and one perfect unity, consent and agreement. . . .

And I believe that this holy Church is catholic, that is to say, that it cannot be . . . restrained within the limits or bonds of any one town, city, province, region, or country; but that it is dispersed and spread universally throughout all the whole world. Insomuch that in what part soever of the world, be it in Africa, Asia, or Europe, there may be found any number of people, of what sort, state, or condition soever they be, which do believe in one God the Father, creator of all things, and in one Lord Jesu Christ his Son, and in one Holy Ghost, and do also profess and have all one faith, one hope, and one charity, according as is prescribed in holy Scripture, and do all consent in the true interpretation of the same Scripture, and in the right use of the sacraments of Christ; we may boldly pronounce and say, that there is this holy Church, the very . . . kingdom of Christ, and the very temple of God.

And I believe that . . . between [these particular churches in different parts of the world] there is indeed no difference in superiority, preeminence, or authority, neither that any one of them is head or sovereign over the other; but that they be all equal in power and dignity, and be all grounded and builded upon one foundation, and be all . . . subject unto one God, one Lord, one head Jesu Christ, and be all governed with one holy spirit. And therefore I do believe that the church of Rome is not, nor cannot worthily be called the catholic Church, but only a particular member thereof and cannot challenge or vindicate of right, and by the word of God, to be head of this universal Church, or to have any superiority over the other churches of Christ which be in England, France, Spain, or in any other realm, but that they be all free from any subjection unto the said church of Rome. . . .

And I believe also that . . . the unity of this one catholic Church is a mere spiritual unity, consisting in the points before rehearsed. . . . And therefore although the said particular churches and the members of the same do much differ . . . not only in the diversity of nations and countries, and in the diversity, dignity, and excellency of certain such gifts of the Holy Ghost as they be endued with, but also in the divers using and observation of such outward rites, ceremonies, traditions, and ordinances as be instituted by their governors . . . ; yet I believe assuredly that the unity of this catholic Church cannot therefore . . . [be] infringed in any point, but that all the said churches do and shall continue still in the unity of this catholic Church, notwithstanding any such diversity. . . . And I believe that all the particular churches in the world, which be members of this catholic Church, may all be called apostolical churches, as well as the church of Rome, or any other church, wherein the apostles themselves were sometime resident; forasmuch as they have received and be all founded upon the same faith and doctrine that the true apostles of Christ did teach and profess. . . . (pp. 52-6)

(II) [from] *The exposition of the Sacrament of Orders* . . . the office of preaching is the chief and most principal office, whereunto priests or bishops be called by the authority of the gospel. . . . (p. 109)

. . . [the] pretended monarchy of the Bishop of Rome is not founded upon the gospel, but it is repugnant thereto. And therefore it appertaineth unto Christian kings and princes . . . to reform . . . [the Church of Christ] again unto the old limits and pristine state of that power and jurisdiction which was given unto them by Christ, and used in the primitive Church. For it is out of all doubt that Christ's faith was then most firm and pure, and the Scriptures of God were then best understanded, and virtue did then most abound and excel. (pp. 121-2)

[*The expositions of the Seven Sacraments* end:] . . . although the sacraments of matrimony, of confirmation, of holy orders, and of extreme unction, have been of long time past received and approved by the common consent of the catholic Church, to have the name and dignity of sacraments, as indeed they be well worthy to have; . . . yet there is a difference in dignity and necessity between them and the other three sacraments . . . of baptism, of penance, and of the altar and that for divers causes. First, because these three sacraments be instituted of Christ, to be as certain instruments or remedies necessary for our salvation. . . . Second, because they be also commanded by Christ to be ministered and received in their outward visible signs. Thirdly, because they have annexed and conjoined unto their said visible signs such spiritual graces, as whereby our sins be remitted and forgiven, and we be perfectly renewed . . . justified and made the very members of Christ's mystical body, so oft as we worthily and duly receive the same. (pp. 128-9)

(III) . . . *The exposition of the Second Commandment* [begins by repeating the precepts given in Articles VI, VII and VIII of the Ten Articles (2 above) and continues:] And they also that be more ready with their substance to deck dead images gorgeously and gloriously, than with the same to help poor Christian people, the quick and lively images of God, which is the necessary work of charity, commanded by God; and they also that so dote in this behalf, that they make vows, and go on pilgrimages even to the images, and there do call upon the same images for aid and help, phantasying that either the image will work . . . or God for the image's sake, as though God wrought by images carved, engraven, or painted, brought once into churches, as he doth work by other his creatures. In which things, if any person heretofore hath or yet doth offend, all good and well learned men have great cause to lament such error and rudeness. . . . (pp. 137-8)

[*The expositions of the Ten Commandments* end with 'notes necessary to be learned' for their better understanding – these include the following:] . . . our Saviour Christ reduceth all these ten commandments unto two commandments, belonging to the heart, that is to say, to the love of God and our neighbour. For whereas the Pharisees came unto Christ and said, Master, which is the greatest commandment of the law? our Saviour answered them and said: The chief and greatest commandment is, that thou shalt love thy Lord God with all thy heart, with all thy soul, and with all thy mind. And the second, like to this, is, that thou shalt love thy neighbour even as thyself. And in these two commandments standeth and consisteth all the whole law and the prophets. . . . (p. 174)

[IV In the section on the Paternoster, stress is laid not only on the paramount importance of loving and honouring 'our most heavenly Father' but on the need for a preaching of the word which 'may so work and feed every part of us, that it may appear in all the acts and deeds of our life'. (p. 189)]

Institution of a Christian Man (1537), printed in
Formularies of Faith, ed. Charles Lloyd (1825)

V

DISSOLUTION OF THE MONASTERIES

1 Extract from the *Valor Ecclesiasticus* (1535), relating to the Benedictine Monastery of Peterborough

In January 1535, shortly after the passing of the Act annexing First fruits* and Tenths to the Crown (**III, 9**), commissioners were sent to every diocese to assess in detail all ecclesiastical incomes, both spiritual and temporal. Their returns were made within six to seven months, the final record being known as the *Valor Ecclesiasticus*. The *Valor*, which superseded the 1291 valuation of Pope Nicholas IV, was a remarkable administrative achievement; the printed edition (1810-34) fills six large folio volumes. It is clear that the returns underestimated some ecclesiastical incomes. The net annual income of the houses included in the *Valor* (a few are missing) was assessed at £136,361. As well as acquiring a very large income by the subsequent Dissolution, the Crown gained a great deal from the sale of monastic plate and other valuables.

The Benedictine monastery of Peterborough was one of the wealthiest houses. Its buildings were used after the Dissolution for the new Cathedral of Peterborough, the last abbot becoming the first bishop. Only twenty-four houses listed in the *Valor* had a net income of over £1,000; these were nearly all Benedictine.

As with other valuations made at that time, there are a few arithmetical errors in the following extract.

THE MONASTERY OF PETERBOROUGH	£ s. d.	£ s. d.

Lordships, manors, lands and possessions lying and being in the several following counties and belonging to the monastery of Peterborough aforesaid, of which John Borough is the abbot, namely in:

THE COUNTY OF NORTHAMPTON   £ s. d.   £ s. d.

[Annual] Value:

TEMPORALITIES

The site of the monastery of Peterborough aforesaid, with the curtilage [court or yard], gardens, orchards, and divers houses, situate within the precincts ... and also the demesne lands, meadows and pastures being in the hands of the abbot and convent, with the tenths of the same demesne lands assessed by the king's commissioners as is contained fully in the declaration made therein   .   .   .   55 3 10

Rents of assize with the rents and farms of tenants in divers lordships, vills, hamlets and parishes in the same viz:

[THE ABBOT'S DEMESNE]

	£	s.	d.
The Lordship of Peterborough . .	70	6	8
Boroughbury	63	15	1½
Eye	63	3	10
Thorpe	41	3	10
Castor	34	9	2½
Werrington . . .	35	19	2
Walton	16	1	8
Glinton	57	13	8½
Stamford [Baron] . . .	18	14	4
Kettering	97	8	9¾
Irthlingborough . . .	33	8	1½
Stanwick	21	15	6½
Oundle	88	18	0½
Ashton	21	16	10
Warmington . . .	49	6	5¼
Cottingham . . .	45	17	4
The hundred of Nassaburgh .	15	0	5¾
The hundred of Polebrook & Navisford	10	18	1½
The hundred of Huxloe . .	11	18	0½
[Total	797	15	3¾]

[Then is listed 'The Portion of the Con- £ s. d.   £ s. d
vent', i.e. the rents etc. received from his
estates by every conventual officer, e.g. the
cellarer, sacrist, almoner, bursar, etc. The
highest number of estates held by an officer
was five; several held one only, generally
in the vill of Peterborough itself.]

                    [Total 208 2 4¼.]
                                            1005 17 6¼

[Incomes from mills, tolls, markets, woods,
fines and 'perquisites of courts and other
amercements'] .   .   .   . .[127 9 3⅛]
[Grand total of Temporalities in the
County of Northampton] .   .   .   1088 10 7⅜
                                       [*1188 10 7⅜*]

SPIRITUALITIES
Profits from:
Oundle rectory, leased by indenture to
    Robert Baker 54 6 8
Warmington rectory, assessed with the
    cellarer's office, leased to Miles Forest 34 0 0
Maxey rectory 13 16 8
Gunthorpe, the tithe* of sheaves of corn
    therefrom, assessed with the almoner's
    office 11 0 0
The vill of Burgh, the tithe of sheaves of
    corn therefrom, assessed with the sac-
    rist's office, leased to William Alger, 18 0 0
    and   .   .   .   .   .
Eye, the tithe of sheaves of corn in this
    hamlet, assessed with [the office of]
    the warden of Oxney .   .   .   5 0 0
as is clear from our examination of the
    said declaration thereon   .   136 3 4
[Other 'pensions and portions [of tithes]
with divers offerings and other profits' in
Northamptonshire follow, amounting to
£45 12s. 8d. 45 12 8

This brings the total Spiritualities in Northamptonshire to £181 16s. 0d.

	£ s. d.	£ s. d.
Total of annual value in Northampton-shire		1370 6 7⅛
Then are listed further payments (mostly temporalities) from the counties of Rutland, Leicestershire, Huntingdonshire, Lincolnshire, Nottinghamshire and Middlesex, amounting to]		[609 0 10½]
[Gross annual revenue of the monastery – Spiritualities and Temporalities] . .		1979 7 5⅝

[There follows a long list of deductions allowed by the commissioners out of both temporalities and spiritualities, for rents, 'fees paid annually to divers officers' (bailiffs, stewards, etc.), annual pensions, and permanent alms. These totalled £257 13s. 5d.]

	£ s. d.
And there remains	1721 14 0⅝
From which for tenths	172 3 5

[A few other deductions are now made for further fees and alms, and for money 'paid annually for five hundred pounds of wax, used in the chancel'.]

	£ s. d.
Leaving a clear balance of	**1679 15 8⅝**

The Last Days of Peterborough Monastery, ed. W. T. Mellows (*Northamptonshire Record Society*, xii, 1947) pp. 4–20 *passim*, being a translation from *Valor Ecclesiasticus*, ed. J. Caley and J. Hunter (1810–34), iv.279–84

2   (a) (b) and (c) Letters to Cromwell from the monastic visitors, 1535

In the summer of 1535 Cromwell, as vicegerent, sent out commissioners to carry out a visitation of religious houses, whose revenue was now largely known to him as a result of the *Valor*. Whilst his ostensible object was reform, Cromwell aimed to compile an unfavourable report for submission to the Parliament of 1536. Some of his visitors were unpleasant and derisive, believing or affecting to believe all the charges they heard; others were more fair-minded and objective. Whilst by no means all reports were derogatory, distortion was not necessarily present in all those which were: some of the criticisms can be supported by reference to recent episcopal visitations of monasteries. Several visitors kept in touch with Cromwell by letter: three examples follow.

The Injunctions issued by the visitors after each visitation often strongly deprecated relics. With his letter of 24 August 1535 (2(a)) Dr. Layton sent Cromwell the relics he found at Maiden Bradley Priory, Wiltshire, and at Bruton Abbey, Somerset. The houses referred to in 2(b) were in Oxfordshire and Northants.

(a) DR RICHARD LAYTON TO CROMWELL, 24 AUGUST 1535

By this bringer my servant, I send you relics; first, two flowers wrapped in white and black sarcenet that on Christmas eve, [in the hour on which Christ was born], will spring and burgeon and bear blossoms, [which may be put to the test], saith the prior of Maiden Bradley: ye shall also receive a bag of relics, wherein ye shall see strange things, as shall appear by the Scripture, as, God's coat, Our Lady's smock, part of God's supper . . . , [part of the stone of the manger in which was born Jesus in Bethlehem]; belike there is in Bethlehem plenty of stones and some quarry, and maketh their mangers of stone. The Scripture of everything shall declare you all; and all this of Maiden Bradley, where is an holy father prior and hath but 6 children, and but one daughter married yet of the goods of the monastery, trusting shortly to marry the rest. His sons be tall men waiting upon him, and he thanks God he never meddled with married women, but all with maidens the fairest could be got, and always married them right well. The Pope, considering his fragility, gave him licence to keep an whore, and [he] hath good writing . . . to discharge his conscience. . . .

I send you also Our Lady's girdle of Bruton, red silk, which is a solemn relic sent to women travelling, which shall not miscarry [in childbirth]. I send you also Mary Magdalen's girdle, and that is wrapped and covered with white, sent also with great reverence to women travelling, which girdle Matilda the empress . . . gave unto them. . . . I have crosses of silver and gold, some which I send you not now because I have more that shall be delivered me this night by the prior of Maiden Bradley himself. Tomorrow . . . I shall bring you the rest. . . .

Richard Layton

T.C.L., pp. 58-9

(b) JOHN TREGONWELL TO CROMWELL, 27 SEPTEMBER 1535

Pleaseth you to be advertised that after my departing from Oxford I went to Godstow where I found all things well and in good order as well in the monastery . . . , as also in the convent of the same, except that one sister 13 or 14 years past, being then of another house, brake her chastity, . . . the which for correction and punishment afterward was sent to Godstow by the Bishop of Lincoln, where now and ever since that time she hath lived virtuous.

From thence I went to Eynsham where I found a raw sort of religious persons . . . amongst them (almost in all kinds of sin committed . . .); for the which offences they have been punished by their ordinary* in his visitation. Yet by as much as I can perceive, . . . the abbot is chaste of his living and doth right well overlook [supervise] the reparations of his house, to whom I can object nothing but that he is negligent in overseeing his brethren. He saith that his daily infirmity is the occasion thereof, which infirmity somewhat did appear by his face to be true.

From Eynsham to Bruern, where the abbot is (as it appeareth to me) not only virtuous and well learned in holy Scripture, but also hath right well repaired the ruin and decay of that house, left by his predecessors' negligence, and the convent (which heretofore were insolent) being now brought to good order. From Bruern I rode to Wroxton, a house of small rents, and standeth most by husbandry. The prior there, although he be a husband [good manager] and keepeth good hospitality to his ability, yet he is rude and unlearned. . . .

From thence to Clattercote . . . , where I found 3 canons beside the prior. That house is old, foul and filthy. Whether their living be according, I cannot tell, for they desired me that I would not visit them because (as they said) that you had given (by your commission) full authority to the prior of Sempringham [head of the Gilbertine Order] to visit all their order . . .; and because I would not [intervene] without your pleasure to me known, I departed then, [no business done].

And from that house . . . I came to a house of nuns called Catesby, of £90 lands yearly, of the order of Citeaux, under my lord of Lincoln's jurisdiction (as I suppose) by usurpation. For that order as you know hath always been exempt from the Bishop. The prioress there is a right sad matron, the sisters also there now being by the space of 20 years hath been (by as much as I can learn) without suspicion of incontinent living.

From Catesby I rode to Canons Ashby, which house is £160 in debt, by reason of the late preferment of the prior there now being. The house also, by the negligence of his predecessor, is in ruin and decay. Howbeit the said prior (although he be unlearned) is disposed to thrive, and by the learning and good example of . . . the sub-prior . . . the religious men there be like to do well.

From Canons Ashby, I rode to Chacombe; the prior is newly come thither, who is competently well learned in holy Scripture. The canons being rude and unlearned, he beginneth to bring them to some order. I fear nothing in him but negligence and overmuch familiarity, which he useth amongst them.

From Chacombe I came to Bicester; there I find that the prior doth well overlook his brethren, and also the profits of his house. His said brethren by his time hath been in good order, excepted one [who] (. . . afraid of punishment for his incontinent living) ran away, and so he remaineth at this time in apostasy. . . .

> Yours most bounden,
>
> John Tregonwell

To the right honourable Mr. Thomas Cromwell, chief secretary to the

King's Majesty, be this delivered with speed.

Public Record Office, S.P.1/97, pp. 37-8

(c) DR RICHARD LAYTON TO CROMWELL, 22 DECEMBER 1535

It may please your Lordship, to understand, that . . . I appointed to meet with Doctor Legh, first a priory of Gilbertines and nuns enclosed and close [probably Chicksand, Beds.]; whereas they would not in any wise have admitted me as visitor, I would not be so answered, but visited them, and there found two of the said nuns not barren; one of them *impregnavit supprior domus* [pregnant by the sub-prior], and [the] other [by] a serving-man. The two prioresses would not confess this, neither the parties, nor none of the nuns, but one old beldame. . . . Another priory called Harwood [Beds.], wherein was 4 or 5 nuns with the prioress; one of them had two fair children, another one and no more. . . . At S. Andrew's in Northampton the house is in debt greatly, the lands sold and mortgaged, the farms let out, and the rent received beforehand, for 10, 15, 20 chantries founded to be paid out of the lands, and great bonds of forfeitures thereupon for non-payment; the house is [worth] four hundred pounds in revenues. The King's foundation thus to be mangled by the quondam, I have pity; the prior now is a bachelor of divinity, a great husband and a good clerk, and pity it is that ever he came there; if he were promoted to a better thing, and the King's Grace would take it into his hands, so might he recover all the lands again, which the prior shall never. In my return out of the north, I will attempt him so to do, if it be your pleasure. The college of Newark here in Leicester . . ., with an hospital, is well kept, and honest men therein, three hundred pounds in their treasure house before hand. The abbey here is confederate, we suppose, and nothing will confess. The abbot is an honest man and doth very well, but he hath here the most obstinate and factious canons that ever I knew. . . .

By the speedy hand of your assured priest and servant,

Richard Layton

T.C.L., pp. 91-4

3   Act for the Dissolution of the Lesser Monasteries, 1536 (27 Hen. VIII, c. 28)

After receiving a summary of the report of the visitors in February 1536, Parliament passed the following Act. The praise accorded to 'the great and honourable monasteries' seems to indicate that the dissolution of the greater houses was not yet intended.

About 84 of the 327 lesser houses covered by the following Act, including all 17 houses of the Gilbertine Order, obtained exemptions under § XIII, often by purchase of a licence, and were not dissolved until after 1536. The 180 friaries, though poor, were not affected by this Act and were separately dissolved in 1538-9.

By an Act of Parliament in 1536 (27 Hen. VIII, c. 27), the Court of Augmentations was established to administer the ex-monastic properties. This Court for a brief period dominated the financial structure of the State, but in 1554 it was merged into the Exchequer.

Forasmuch as manifest sin, vicious, carnal and abominable living is daily used and committed among the little and small abbeys, priories, and other religious houses of monks, canons, and nuns, where the congregation of such religious persons is under the number of twelve persons, whereby the governors of such religious houses, and their convent, spoil, destroy, consume, and utterly waste, as well their churches, monasteries, priories, principal houses, farms, granges, lands, tenements, and hereditaments, as the ornaments of their churches, and their goods and chattels, to the high displeasure of Almighty God, slander of good religion, and to the great infamy of the King's Highness and the realm, if redress should not be had thereof; and albeit that many continual visitations hath been heretofore had, by the space of two hundred years and more, for an honest and charitable reformation of such unthrifty, carnal and abominable living, yet nevertheless little or none amendment is hitherto had, but their vicious living shamelessly increaseth and augmenteth, and by a cursed custom so rooted and infested, that a great multitude of the religious persons in such small houses do rather choose to rove abroad in apostasy, than to conform them to the observation of good religion; so that without such small houses be utterly suppressed, and the religious persons therein committed to great and honourable monasteries of religion in this realm, where they may be compelled to live religiously, for reformation of their lives, there cannot else be no reformation in this behalf:

In consideration whereof, the King's most Royal Majesty, being

Supreme Head in earth, under God, of the Church of England, daily finding and devising the increase, advancement, and exaltation of true doctrine and virtue in the said Church, to the only glory and honour of God, and the total extirping and destruction of vice and sin, having knowledge that the premises be true, as well by the accounts of his late visitations, as by sundry credible informations, considering also that divers and great solemn monasteries of this realm, wherein, thanks be to God, religion is right well kept and observed, be destitute of such full numbers of religious persons, as they ought and may keep, hath thought good that a plain declaration should be made of the premises, as well to the Lords spiritual and temporal as to other his loving subjects the Commons in this present Parliament assembled: whereupon the said Lords and Commons, by a great deliberation, finally be resolved, that it is and shall be much more to the pleasure of Almighty God, and for the honour of this his realm, that the possessions of such spiritual religious houses, now being spent, spoiled, and wasted for increase and maintenance of sin, should be used and converted to better uses, and the unthrifty religious persons so spending the same to be compelled to reform their lives: and thereupon most humbly desire the King's Highness that it may be enacted by authority of this present Parliament, that his Majesty shall have and enjoy to him and to his heirs for ever, all and singular such monasteries, priories, and other religious houses of monks, canons, and nuns, of what kinds or diversities of habits, rules, or orders soever they be called or named, which have not in lands and tenements, rents, tithes*, portions, and other hereditaments, above the clear yearly value of two hundred pounds; and in like manner shall have and enjoy all the sites and circuits of every such religious houses, and all and singular the manors, granges, meases [messuages], lands, tenements, reversions, rents, services, tithes, pensions, portions, churches, chapels, advowsons, patronages, annuities, rights, entries, conditions, and other hereditaments appertaining or belonging to every such monastery, priory or other religious house, not having, as is aforesaid, above the said clear yearly value of two hundred pounds, in as large and ample manner as the abbots, priors, abbesses, prioresses, or other governors of such monasteries, priories, and other religious houses now have, or ought to have the same in the right of their houses. And that also his Highness shall have to him and to his heirs all and singular such monasteries, abbeys, and priories, which at any time within one year next before the making of this Act have been given and granted to his Majesty by any abbot, prior, abbess,

or prioress, under their convent seals, or that otherwise, have been
suppressed or dissolved, and all and singular the manors, lands, [etc.] ...
to the same monasteries, abbeys, and priories, or to any of them appertaining or belonging; to have and to hold all and singular the premises,
with all their rights, profits, jurisdictions, and commodities, unto the
King's Majesty, and to his heirs and assigns for ever, to do and use
therewith his and their own wills, to the pleasure of Almighty God,
and to the honour and profit of this realm.

*   *   *

IV   Provided always, and be it enacted, that forasmuch as divers of
the chief governors of such religious houses, determining the utter
spoil and destruction of their houses, and dreading the suppressing
thereof, for the maintenance of their detestable lives, have lately fraudu-
elntly and craftily made feoffments [method of conveying land],
estates, gifts, grants, and leases, under their convent seals, or suffered
recoveries [another method of conveying land], of their manors, lands,
tenements, and hereditaments in fee simple, fee tail, for term of life or
lives, or for years, or charged the same with rents or corrodies [origin-
ally a grant of food etc., made by a monastery, now often an annuity
or pension], to the great decay and diminution of their houses; that all
such crafty and fraudulent recoveries, feoffments, estates, gifts, grants,
and leases, and every of them, made by any of the said chief governors
of such religious houses, under the convent seals, within one year
next afore the making of this Act, shall be utterly void and of none
effect. ...

V   And it is also enacted ... that the King's Highness shall have and
enjoy to his own proper use, all the ornaments, jewels, goods, chattels,
and debts, which appertained to any of the chief governors of the said
monasteries or religious houses, in the right of their said monasteries
or houses, at the first day of March in the year of our Lord God 1535
[1536, modern style], or any time since, wheresoever, and to whose
possession soever they shall come or be found, except only such beasts,
grain, and woods, and such other like chattels and revenues, as have
been sold in the said first day of March or since, for the necessary or
reasonable expenses or charges of any of the said monasteries or houses.

*   *   *

VIII   In consideration of which premises to be had to his Highness
and to his heirs, as is aforesaid, his Majesty is pleased and contented, of

his most excellent charity, to provide to every chief head and governor of every such religious house, during their lives, such yearly pensions or benefices as for their degrees and qualities shall be reasonable and convenient; wherein his Highness will have most tender respect to such of the said chief governors as well and truly conserve and keep the goods and ornaments of their houses to the use of his Majesty, without spoil, waste, or embezzling the same; and also his Majesty will ordain and provide that the convents of every such religious house shall have their capacities, if they will, to live honestly and virtuously abroad, and some convenient charity disposed to them toward their living, or else shall be committed to such honourable great monasteries of this realm wherein good religion is observed, as shall be limited by his Highness, there to live religiously during their lives.

IX   And it is ordained . . . that the chief governors and convents of such honourable great monasteries shall take and accept into their houses, from time to time, such number of the persons of the said convents as shall be assigned and appointed by the King's Highness, and keep them religiously, during their lives, within their said monasteries, in like manner and form as the convents of such great monasteries be ordered and kept.

*   *   *

XII   And also the King's Majesty is pleased and contented that it be enacted by authority aforesaid, that his Highness shall satisfy, content, and pay all and singular such just and true debts which are owing to any person or persons by the chief governors of any the said religious houses, in as large and ample manner as the said chief governors should or ought to have done if this Act had never been made.

XIII   Provided always, that the King's Highness, at any time after the making of this Act, may at his pleasure ordain and declare, by his letters patent under his great seal, that such of the said religious houses which his Highness shall not be disposed to have suppressed nor dissolved by authority of this Act, shall still continue, remain, and be in the same body corporate, and in the said essential estate, quality, and condition, as well in possessions as otherwise, as they were afore the making of this Act. . . .

*   *   *

XVII   And further be it enacted . . . that all and singular persons, bodies politic and corporate, to whom the King's Majesty, his heirs or successors, hereafter shall give, grant, let, or demise any site or precinct, with the houses thereupon builded, together with the demesnes of any monasteries, priories, or other religious houses, that shall be dissolved or given to the King's Highness by this Act, and the heirs, successors, executors, and assigns of every such person, body politic and corporate, shall be bounden by authority of this Act, under the penalties hereafter ensuing, to keep, or cause to be kept, an honest continual house and household in the same site or precinct, and to occupy yearly as much of the same demesnes in ploughing and tillage of husbandry, that is to say, as much of the said demesnes which hath been commonly used to be kept in tillage by the governors, abbots, or priors of the same houses, monasteries, or priories, or by their farmer or farmers occupying the same within the time of twenty years next before this Act.

And if any person or persons, bodies politic or corporate, that shall be bounden by this Act, do not keep an honest household, husbandry and tillage, in manner and form as is aforesaid, that then he or they so offending shall forfeit to the King's Highness for every month so offending, six pounds thirteen shillings and fourpence, to be recovered to his use in any of his Courts of record.

* * *

Stat. Realm, iii.575-8

4   (a) and (b) Robert Aske on the Dissolution of the Monasteries

Robert Aske, the leader of the Pilgrimage of Grace (executed July 1537), was a pious and sincere Catholic who upheld the Papal Supremacy and believed that the dissolution of the smaller monasteries was likely to cause real harm in the North. Others joined the rebellion from a complex variety of motives: political, religious, legal and economic.

These extracts are taken from Aske's own account of the rising given in London, where he was subjected to a close examination. The first extract (a) relates to the occasion during the revolt when he had explained to the temporal Lords the viewpoint of the common people of the North; in the second (b) he makes his own general case for the retention of the monasteries. Both accounts (especially the first) reflect a fear prevalent in the North that the dissolution would lead to a decrease in the already limited amount of coin available there. Aske makes this the dominant popular grievance.

(*a*) The Lords temporal . . . [had not] providently ordered and declared to his said Highness the poverty of his realm, and that part specially, and wherein their griefs might ensue, whereby all dangers might have been avoided; for insomuch as in the north parts much of the relief of the commons was by succour of abbeys. . . . And that now the profits of abbeys suppressed, tenths and first fruits* went out of those parts. By occasion whereof, within short space . . . there should be no money nor treasure in those parts, neither the tenant to have to pay his rents to the lord, nor the lord to have money to do the King service withal, for so much as in those parts was neither the presence of his Grace, execution of his laws, nor yet but little recourse of merchandise, so that of necessity the said country should either patyse [make a treaty] with the Scots, or for of very poverty, enforced to make commotions or rebellions. . . . (pp. 335-6)

(*b*) The said Aske sayeth: first, to the Statute of suppressions, he did grudge against the same and so did all the whole country, because the abbeys in the north parts gave great alms to poor men and laudably served God; in which parts of late days they had but small comfort by ghostly [spiritual] teaching. And by occasion of the said suppression the divine service of Almighty God is much minished, great number of masses unsaid, and the blessed consecration of the sacrament now not used and showed in those places, to the distress of the faith, and spiritual comfort to man['s] soul, the temple of God . . . pulled down, the ornaments and relics of the church of God unreverent[ly] used, the tombs and sepulchres of honourable and noble men pulled down and sold, none hospitality now in those places kept, but the farmers [the lay occupiers] for the most part let . . . out the farms of the same houses to other farmers for lucre and advantage to themselves. [Aske now speaks about the undesirability of money going out of the north parts, as in the first extract.] . . . And diverse and many of the said abbeys were in the mountains and desert places, where the people be rude of conditions and not well taught the law of God, and when the said abbeys stood, the said people not only had worldly refreshing in their bodies, but also spiritual refuge both by ghostly living of them and also by spiritual information and preaching; and many their tenants were their feed servants to them, and serving men, well succoured by abbeys; and now not only these tenants and servants . . . knoweth not now where to have any living, but also strangers . . . for none was in these parts denied, neither horsemeat nor man's meat, so that the people was greatly refreshed by the said abbeys, where now they have no such succour; and wherefore the said Statute of suppression was greatly to the decay of the common wealth of that country, and all those parts of all degrees greatly grudged against the same, and yet doth their duty of allegiance. . . .

Also the abbeys was one of the beauties of this realm to all men and strangers passing through the same; also all gentlemen much succoured in their needs with money, their young sons there succoured, and in nunneries their daughters brought up in virtue; . . . and such abbeys as were near the danger of sea banks [were] great maintainers of sea walls and dykes, maintainers and builders of bridges and highways [and] such other things for the common wealth. (pp. 561-2)

'The Pilgrimage of Grace' and 'Aske's examination', ed. Mary Bateson, *English Historical Review*, v (1890)

5   Abbot Pyle's Surrender of Furness Abbey, Lancashire (5 April 1537)

During the years 1537-9, many of the greater abbeys surrendered to the King on their own initiative, the first being the Cistercian Abbey of Furness. Such deeds of surrender seem often to have been drawn up by Cromwell's agents. Abbot Pyle signed his surrender at Whalley Abbey, Lancashire, one of the six houses declared forfeit to the Crown by the attainder of their heads for participation in the Pilgrimage of Grace. Pyle himself was in a dangerous position since some of his monks had expressed their sympathy with the rebels.

I, Roger, abbot of the monastery of Furness, knowing the misorder and evil life both unto God and our Prince of the brethren of the said monastery, in discharging of my conscience do freely and wholly surrender, give, and grant unto the King's Highness, and to his heirs and assigns for evermore, all such interest and title as I have had, have, or may have, of and in the said monastery of Furness, and of and in the lands, rents, possessions, revenues, services both spiritual and temporal, and of and in all goods and chattels and all other thing whatsoever it be, belonging or in any wise appertaining to the said monastery and every part and parcel thereof, in as large and ample manner and form as ever I had or ought to have, of and in the same or any part or parcel thereof by any manner of means, title, interest, gift, grant, or otherwise, permitting and binding myself by these presents that from henceforth I shall at all times and in all places, whensoever I shall be called upon, be ready and glad to confirm, ratify, and establish this my deed, purpose, mind, and intent, as shall be devised by the learned Council of the King's said Highness, which cometh freely of myself and without any enforcement, in consideration of the evil disposition of the brethren of the said monastery, as is aforesaid; in witness whereof hereunto I have subscribed my name, and written this bill with mine own [hand] . . . in the presence of the right honourable lord, my lord the Earl of Sussex, the King's Lieutenant within this county of Lancaster, and also in the presence of Sir Thomas Butler, Sir William Leyland, Mr. John Clayden, clerk, Sir John Beron, and Sir Antony Fitzherbert, one of the King's justices, being of the King's Council within the said county, who hereunto have also put to their hands to testify the same.

Per me, Roger, Abbot of Furness
[Five other signatures follow.]

T.C.L., pp. 153-4

6 Act for the Dissolution of the Greater Monasteries, 1539 (31 Hen. VIII, c. 13)

The following Act confirmed the process of surrender outlined in 5 above and also vested all monastic property in the King. The last house to make its surrender was Waltham Abbey, on 23 March 1540.

Where divers and sundry abbots, priors, abbesses, prioresses, and other ecclesiastical governors and governesses of divers monasteries, abbacies, priories, nunneries, colleges, hospitals, houses of friars, and other religious and ecclesiastical houses and places within this our Sovereign Lord the King's realm of England and Wales, of their own free and voluntary minds, good wills and assents, without constraint, coaction, or compulsion of any manner of person or persons, since the fourth day of February, the twenty-seventh year of the reign of our now most dread Sovereign Lord [1536], by the due order and course of the common laws of this his realm of England, and by their sufficient writings of record, under their convent and common seals, have severally given, granted, and by the same their writings severally confirmed all their said monasteries, [etc.] . . . and all their sites, circuits, and precincts of the same, and all and singular their manors, lordships, granges, meases, lands, tenements, meadows, pastures, rents, reversions, services, woods, tithes*, pensions, portions, churches, chapels, advowsons, patronages, annuities, rights, entries, conditions, commons, leets, courts, liberties, privileges, and franchises appertaining or in any wise belonging to any such monastery [etc.] . . . by whatsoever name or corporation they or any of them were then named or called, and of what order, habit, religion, or other kind or quality soever they or any of them then were reputed, known or taken; to have and to hold all the said monasteries [etc.] . . . sites, circuits [etc.] . . . and all other the premises, to our said Sovereign Lord, his heirs and successors for ever, and the same their said monasteries [etc.] . . . sites, circuits [etc.] . . . and other the premises, voluntarily, as is aforesaid, have renounced, left, and forsaken, and every of them hath renounced, left and forsaken:

Be it therefore enacted . . . that the King our Sovereign Lord shall have, hold, possess, and enjoy to him, his heirs and successors for ever, all and singular such late monasteries [etc.] . . . which since the said fourth day of February, the twenty-seventh year of the reign of our said Sovereign Lord, have been dissolved, suppressed, renounced, relinquished, forfeited, given up, or by any other mean come to his Highness; and by the same authority, and in like manner, shall have, hold, possess, and enjoy all the sites [etc.] . . . and other whatsoever hereditaments, which appertained or belonged to the said late monasteries [etc.] . . . or to any of them, in as large and ample manner and form as the late abbots, priors, abbesses, prioresses, and other ecclesiastical governors and governesses of such late monasteries [etc.] . . . had, held, or occupied, or of right ought to have had, holden or occupied, in the rights of their said late monasteries [etc.] . . . at the time of the said dissolution, suppression, renouncing, relinquishing, forfeiting, giving up, or by any other manner of mean coming of the same to the King's Highness since the fourth day of February above specified.

II And it is further enacted . . . that not only all the said late monasteries [etc.] . . . sites [etc.] . . . and all other the premises, forthwith, immediately, and presently, but also all other monasteries [etc.] . . . which hereafter shall happen to be dissolved, suppressed [etc.] . . .; and also all the sites [etc.] . . . and other hereditaments whatsoever they be, belonging or appertaining to the same or any of them, whensoever and as soon as they shall be dissolved [etc.] . . . shall be vested, deemed, and adjudged by authority of this present Parliament, in the very actual and real seisin and possession of the King our Sovereign Lord, his heirs and successors for ever, in the state and condition as they now be; and as though all the said late monasteries [etc.] . . . as also the said monasteries [etc.] . . . which hereafter shall happen to be dissolved, suppressed [etc.] . . . sites [etc.] . . . and other the premises, whatsoever they be, and every of them, were in this present Act specially and particularly rehearsed, named, and expressed by express words, names, titles, and faculties, and in their natures, kinds, and qualities.

III   And be it also enacted . . . that all the said late monasteries [etc.] . . . which be dissolved, [etc.] . . . and all the manors, lordships, granges, lands, tenements, and other the premises, except such thereof as be come to the King's hands by attainder or attainders of treason, and all the said monasteries [etc.] . . . which hereafter shall happen to be dissolved [etc.] . . . and all the manors, lordships, granges, lands, tenements, meadows, pastures, rents, reversions, services, woods, tithes, portions, pensions, parsonages, appropriate* vicarages, churches, chapels, advowsons, nominations, patronages, annuities, rights, interests, entries, conditions, commons, leets, courts, liberties, privileges, franchises, and other hereditaments, whatsoever they be, belonging to the same, or to any of them, except such thereof which shall happen to come to the King's Highness by attainder or attainders of treason, shall be in the order, survey, and governance of our said Sovereign Lord the King's Court of Augmentations of the Revenues of his Crown. . . .

*   *   *

XVIII   And be it further enacted . . . that such of the said late monasteries [etc.] . . . and all churches and chapels to them or any of them belonging, which before the dissolution, suppression [etc.] . . . were exempted from the visitation or visitations, and all jurisdiction of the ordinary* or ordinaries within whose diocese they were situate or set, shall from henceforth be within the jurisdiction and visitation of the ordinary or ordinaries within whose diocese they or any of them be situate and set, or within the jurisdiction and visitation of such person or persons as by the King's Highness shall be limited or appointed; this Act, or any other exemption, liberty, or jurisdiction to the contrary notwithstanding.

*   *   *

VI

THE LAST YEARS OF
HENRY VIII, 1539-47

1 The Act of Six Articles, 1539 (31 Hen. VIII, c. 14)

Early in May 1539 a committee of the House of Lords was appointed to decide on the best means of abolishing diversity in religion, but before it had been given adequate time to make proposals, the Duke of Norfolk announced that the King desired the House to consider six articles of doctrine. After a disputation in which opposition came from Archbishop Cranmer, Nicholas Shaxton of Salisbury and Hugh Latimer of Worcester, a bill incorporating the articles was introduced into the Lords on 7 June. By 16 June it had passed both Houses. This statement of traditional beliefs, denial of any of which was made penal, proceeded not from the Church (though it was sanctioned by Convocation) but from Parliament acting on the King's orders. Those who leaned toward Protestant doctrine saw the Act as a major defeat, Shaxton and Latimer resigning their sees.

In the preamble reference is made to communion in both kinds. Whereas by custom the priest had taken both bread and wine, the laity taking the bread only, all the leading Protestant theologians regarded this restriction as unjustified by Scripture or by early Christian practice. See also **3** below and **VII, 1**.

The severity of §§ XX and XXI was mitigated by an amendment of 1540 under which priests and women twice convicted of concubinage were exempted from the death penalty.

Where the King's most excellent Majesty is, by God's law, Supreme Head immediately under Him of this whole Church and Congregation of England, intending the conservation of the same Church and Congregation in a true, sincere, and uniform doctrine of Christ's religion, calling also to his blessed and most gracious remembrance as well the great and quiet assurance, prosperous increase, and other innumerable commodities, which have ever ensued, come and followed, of con-

cord, agreement, and unity in opinions, as also the manifold perils,
dangers, and inconveniences which have heretofore, in many places
and regions, grown, sprung, and arisen, of the diversities of minds and
opinions especially of matters of Christian religion, and therefore desiring that such a unity might and should be charitably established in
all things touching and concerning the same, as the same, so being
established, might chiefly be to the honour of Almighty God, the very
author and fountain of all true unity and sincere concord, and consequently redound to the common wealth of this his Highness's most
noble realm, and of all his loving subjects, and other residents and
inhabitants of or in the same; hath therefore caused and commanded
this his most High Court of Parliament, for sundry and many urgent
causes and considerations, to be at this time summoned, and also a
Synod and Convocation of all the archbishops, bishops and other
learned men of the clergy of this his realm, to be in like manner
assembled.

And forasmuch as in the said Parliament, Synod, and Convocation,
there were certain articles, matters and questions proponed and set
forth touching Christian religion . . .

The King's most Royal Majesty, most prudently pondering and considering, that by occasion of variable and sundry opinions and judgments of the said articles, great discord and variance has arisen, as well
amongst the clergy of this his realm, as amongst a great number of
vulgar people, his loving subjects of the same, and being in a full hope
and trust that a full and perfect resolution of the said articles should
make a perfect concord and unity generally amongst all his loving and
obedient subjects, of his most excellent goodness, not only commanded
that the said articles should deliberately and advisedly, by his said
archbishops, bishops and other learned men of his clergy, be debated,
argued, and reasoned, and their opinions therein to be understood, declared, and known, but also most graciously vouchsafed, in his own
princely person, to descend and come into his said High Court of
Parliament and Council, and there, like a prince of most high prudence
and no less learning, opened and declared many things of high learning
and great knowledge, touching the said articles, matters and questions,
for a unity to be had in the same; whereupon, after a great and long,
deliberate, and advised disputation and consultation . . . as well by the
consent of the King's Highness, as by the assent of the Lords spiritual
and temporal, and other learned men of his clergy in their Convoca-

tion, and by the consent of the Commons in this present Parliament assembled, it was and is finally resolved, accorded and agreed in manner and form following, that is to say:

First, that in the most blessed sacrament of the altar, by the strength and efficacy of Christ's mighty word, it being spoken by the priest, is present really, under the form of bread and wine, the natural body and blood of our Saviour Jesus Christ, conceived of the Virgin Mary; and that after the consecration there remaineth no substance of bread or wine, nor any other substance but the substance of Christ, God and man.

Secondly, that communion in both kinds is not necessary *ad salutem*, by the law of God, to all persons; and that it is to be believed, and not doubted of, but that in the flesh under form of bread is the very blood, and with the blood under form of wine is the very flesh, as well apart as though they were both together.

Thirdly, that priests after the order of priesthood received, as afore, may not marry by the law of God.

Fourthly, that vows of chastity or widowhood, by man or woman made to God advisedly, ought to be observed by the law of God, and that it exempteth them from other liberties of Christian people, which without that they might enjoy.

Fifthly, that it is meet and necessary that private masses be continued and admitted in this the King's English Church and Congregation, as whereby good Christian people, ordering themselves accordingly, do receive both godly and goodly consolations and benefits, and it is agreeable also to God's law.

Sixthly, that auricular confession is expedient and necessary to be retained and continued, used and frequented in the Church of God.

For the which most godly study, pain, and travail of his Majesty, and determination and resolution of the premises, his most humble and obedient subjects, the Lords spiritual and temporal and the Commons in this present Parliament assembled, not only render and give unto his Highness their most high and hearty thanks, and think themselves most bounden to pray for the long continuance of his Grace's most royal estate, but also being desirous that his most godly enterprise may be well accomplished, and brought to a full end and perfection, and so established that the same might be to the honour of God, and after to the common quiet, unity and concord to be had in the whole body of this realm forever, most humbly beseech his Royal Majesty, that the resolution and determination above written of the said articles may be established, and perpetually perfected, by authority of this present Parliament:

It is therefore ordained and enacted . . .

[I   Any who, after 12 July 1539 by word, writing or printing, declare anything contrary to the first article, or who 'despise the said blessed sacrament' shall, together with their supporters, be guilty of heresy and burned.

II   Any who preach or teach, or upon trial 'obstinately affirm' contrary to the other five articles, or any man or woman who, having vowed chastity, shall marry, shall suffer a felon's death.

III   Any who shall otherwise 'publish declare or hold opinion' contrary to articles ii–vi shall suffer imprisonment and loss of all property for the first offence, and a felon's death for a second offence.

IV   Marriages of priests and of persons who have 'vowed chastity or widowhood . . . shall be utterly void'.

*   *   *

VI   Any who 'contemptuously refuse, deny, or abstain to be confessed at the time commonly accustomed . . . or abstain to receive the holy and blessed sacrament' at the time commonly accustomed shall suffer imprisonment and pay a fine; a second offence to be felony.

VII and VIII   For 'full and effectual execution of the premises', special periodic commissions shall be instituted. Also, those having ecclesiastical jurisdiction and justices of the peace and certain others, are empowered to enquire into offences under the Act.

*   *   *

XVII   The commissioners shall 'have full power and authority' to 'burn or otherwise destroy' any books containing matter 'repugnant or contrary' to the Act.

XVIII   Parish priests shall periodically read the Act in their churches.

*   *   *

XX and XXI   After 12 July 1539, any priest convicted of concubinage shall suffer imprisonment, forfeiture of goods and deprivation for the first offence, and a felon's death for a second; the women involved 'shall have like punishment'.]

★　　★　　★

Stat. Realm, iii.739-43

2   Cranmer's Preface to the Great Bible, 1540

In addition to his famous New Testament (see **II, 4, 5**), Tyndale published translations of the Pentateuch and *Jonah*, but his gifted disciple Miles Coverdale was responsible for the first complete printed Bible in English, published abroad in 1535. (Coverdale's fine version of the Psalms is still in use as part of the Anglican *Book of Common Prayer*.) In 1535 the Southwark printer James Nicholson gained permission to issue Coverdale's Bible in England. Two years later Richard Grafton was allowed to print the 'Matthew Bible', a translation by John Rogers (*alias* Thomas Matthew), chaplain to the English merchants at Antwerp and later the first of the Marian martyrs. All these versions remained deeply indebted to Tyndale's, while in every case effective support came from Thomas Cromwell, who had in fact taken a personal interest in Coverdale's translation-schemes as early as 1527. It will be remembered that Cromwell's Injunctions of 1538 (**IV, 4**) order every parson to provide an English Bible in his church, with free access to readers. In the same year Cromwell decided to sponsor an authoritative revision, entrusting the work to Coverdale, who considerably revised his own previous translation whilst drawing also on other translations. Grafton and his partner Whitchurch began printing this 'Great Bible' in Paris, but were compelled to flee by the Inquisitor General, and they completed their work in England. The Great Bible appeared in April 1539 and had achieved six further editions by the end of 1541. Rather inappropriately, it became known as Cranmer's Bible, because of this preface appended by the Archbishop to the second and subsequent editions. Various other translations of the Bible were made in the second half of the century, culminating in the 'Authorized Version' in the reign of James I. This drew on many sources but still owed a very great deal to Tyndale.

Hitherto, all that I have said, I have taken and gathered out of the foresaid sermon of this holy doctor, St. John Chrysostom [*c.* 347-407]. Now if I should in like manner bring forth what the self-same doctor speaketh in other places, and what other doctors and writers say concerning the same purpose, I might seem to you to write another Bible rather than to make a preface to the Bible. Wherefore, in few words to comprehend the largeness and utility of the Scripture, how it containeth fruitful instruction and erudition for every man; if any thing be necessary to be learned, of the holy Scripture we may learn it. If falsehood shall be reproved, thereof we may gather wherewithal. If any thing be to be corrected and amended, if there need any exhortation or consolation, of the Scripture we may well learn. In the Scriptures be the fat pastures of the soul; therein is no venomous meat, no unwholesome thing; they be the very dainty and pure feeding. He that is ignorant, shall find there what he should learn. He that is a perverse sinner, shall there find his damnation to make him to tremble for fear. He that laboureth to serve God, shall find there his glory, and the promissions of eternal life, exhorting him more diligently to labour. Herein may princes learn how to govern their subjects; subjects, obedience, love and dread to their princes: husbands, how they should behave them unto their wives; how to educate their children and servants: and contrary, the wives, children, and servants may know their duty to their husbands, parents and masters. Here may all manner of persons, ... of what estate or condition soever they be ... learn all things what they ought to believe, what they ought to do, and what they should not do, as well concerning Almighty God, as also concerning themselves and all other. Briefly, to the reading of the Scripture none can be enemy, but that either be so sick that they love not to hear of any medicine, or else that be so ignorant that they know not Scripture to be the most healthful medicine.

Therefore, as touching this former part, I will here conclude and take it as a conclusion sufficiently determine[d] and appoint[ed], that it is convenient and good the Scripture to be read of all sorts and kinds of people, and in the vulgar tongue, without further allegations and probations for the same; which shall not need, since that this one place of John Chrysostom is enough and sufficient to persuade all them that be not frowardly and perversely set in their own wilful opinion; specially now that the King's Highness, being Supreme Head next under Christ of this Church of England, hath approved with his royal assent the setting forth hereof, which only to all true and obedient subjects ought to be a sufficient reason for the allowance of the same, without farther delay, reclamation, or resistance, although there were no preface nor other reason herein expressed.

Therefore now to come to the second and latter part of my purpose. There is nothing so good in this world, but it may be abused, and turned from fruitful and wholesome to hurtful and noisome. What is there above better, than the sun, the moon, the stars? Yet was there that took occasion by the great beauty and virtue of them to dishonour God, and to defile themselves with idolatry, giving the honour of the living God and Creator of all things to such things as he had created. What is there here beneath better than fire, water, meats, drinks, metals of gold, silver, iron, and steel? Yet we see daily great harm and much mischief done by every one of these, as well for lack of wisdom and providence of them that suffer evil, as by the malice of them that worketh the evil. Thus to them that be evil of themselves everything setteth forward and increaseth their evil, be it of his own nature a thing never so good; like as contrarily, to them that studieth and endeavoureth themselves to goodness, every thing prevaileth them, and profiteth unto good, be it of his own nature a thing never so bad. As St. Paul saith: *His qui diligunt Deum, omnia cooperantur in bonum* ['To them that love God all things work together for good' (*Romans*, viii.28).]: even as out of most venomous worms is made triacle [an antidote], the most sovereign medicine for the preservation of man's health in time of danger. Wherefore I would advise you all, that cometh to the reading or hearing of this book, which is the word of God, the most precious jewel and most holy relic that remaineth upon earth, that ye bring with you the fear of God, and that ye do it with all due reverence, and use your knowledge thereof, not to vain-glory of frivolous disputation, but to the honour of God, increase of virtue, and edification both of yourselves and other.

> *Miscellaneous Writings and Letters of Thomas Cranmer*, ed. J. E. Cox (*Parker Society*, 1846) pp. 121-2

3   Extracts from the *King's Book* (*A Necessary Doctrine and Erudition for any Christian Man*), 1543

This was a revision by a committee of divines of the *Bishops' Book* (**IV, 5**). The King fully authorised it and wrote the preface: thus it became known as the *King's Book*. Apart from a strong repudiation of the 'pretensed universal primacy' of the Bishop of Rome, the presentation of doctrine is in large part traditional, orthodox, and sometimes pointedly anti-Lutheran. On the other hand, the attitude of the years 1536-8 has not been entirely laid aside. A definition of the word 'purgatory'* is still avoided; the admonition in the *Bishops' Book* against those that 'deck images gorgeously' is repeated. In the 'Article of Justification', the gradualist Augustinian view of the justificatory process is emphasised, i.e. to be made righteous by grace is a life-long process in which man's good works play a necessary part. Nevertheless, these are preferably to be 'all inward spiritual works', while the 'superstitious works of men's own invention' are proscribed.

The reference in the preface to the restraint imposed on the reading of the Bible is to the Act for the advancement of True Religion, 1543 (34 and 35 Hen. VIII, c. 1). This Act forbade the use of Tyndale's 'crafty, false and untrue' translation of the Bible and of 'all other books . . . teaching or comprising any matters of Christian religion . . . contrary to the doctrines set forth by the King' since 1540, and limited the reading of the authorised translation of the Bible to certain classes only (nobles, gentry, clergy and substantial merchants). The Act seems to have proved ineffectual.

[In his preface the King declares that latterly there had 'entered into some of our people's hearts an inclination to sinister understanding of Scripture, presumption, arrogancy, carnal liberty, and contention'. It is therefore necessary to set forth such 'declaration of the true knowledge of God and his word . . . as whereby all men may uniformly be led and taught the true understanding of that which is necessary for every Christian man to know'. Although it is clearly necessary for those who teach the Scriptures to read and study them, judgment as to whether the people should do so must rest with 'the prince and the policy of the realm'. 'Consonant whereunto the politic law of our realm hath now restrained it [the Bible] from a great many, esteeming it sufficient for those so restrained to hear and truly bear away the doctrine of Scripture taught by the preachers.' (pp. 215-9)]

The Sacrament of the Altar

[This passage clearly upholds transubstantiation* and includes the following:] For the benefit or hurt that cometh to a Christian man by receiving of this sacrament standeth not in the fashion or manner of receiving of it, under one or both kinds, but in the worthy or unworthy receiving of the same. For he that receiveth this sacrament worthily under the one kind, as under the form of bread only, receiveth the whole body and blood of Christ, and as many and great benefits of

Christ as he that receiveth it in both kinds. And therefore if any man should teach that the lay people (which by the ordinance and ancient custom of the catholic Church have used to receive this holy sacrament in form of bread only) be seduced and so cause them to think that the whole body and blood of Christ were not comprehended in that only form of bread, as well as in both the kinds, this doctrine ought utterly to be refused ... as a pestiferous and a devilish school. ... (pp. 265-6)

The Article of Freewill
The commandments and threatenings of Almighty God in Scripture, whereby man is called upon and put in remembrance what God would have him to do, most evidently do express and declare that man hath freewill also now after the fall of our first father Adam, as plainly appeareth in these places following: Be not overcome of evil. Neglect not the grace that is in thee. ... If thou wilt enter into life, keep the commandments. Which undoubtedly should be said in vain, unless there were some faculty or power left in man whereby he may, by the help and grace of God (if he will receive it when it is offered unto him), understand his commandments and freely consent and obey unto them. ... Freewill is a power of reason and will, by which good is chosen by the assistance of grace, or evil is chosen without the assistance of the same.

[Man's 'condition of freewill' is very greatly diminished from that which Adam and Eve enjoyed before the Fall. By their transgression the degree of freewill, both in themselves and in all their posterity, became 'weak and feeble' and of no avail 'in spiritual desires and works to please God' unless helped by the grace of God.]

... it followeth that freewill, before it may will or think any godly thing, must be holpen by the grace of Christ ... [and] may from thenceforth work together with grace and by the same sustained, holpen, and maintained, may do and accomplish good works, and avoid sin, and persevere also and increase in grace. ...

All men be also to be monished, and chiefly preachers, that in this high matter they looking on both sides, so attemper and moderate themselves, that neither they so preach the grace of God that they take away thereby freewill, nor on the other side so extol freewill, that injury be done to the grace of God. (pp. 359-63)

The Article of Justification

... this word justification, as it is taken in Scripture, signifieth the making of us righteous afore God. ... And albeit God is the principal cause and chief worker of this justification in us, without whose grace no man can do no good thing ... yet so it pleaseth the high wisdom of God, that man ... shall be also a worker by his free consent and obedience ... in the attaining of his own justification, and by God's grace and help shall walk in such works as be requisite to his justification. ...

Wherein it is to be considered, that although our Saviour Christ hath offered himself upon the cross a sufficient redemption and satisfaction for the sins of the world ... [and] calleth upon all the world, without respect of persons, to come and be partakers of the righteousness, peace, and glory which is in him; yet ... none shall have the effect of this benefit of our Saviour Christ, and enjoy everlasting salvation by him, but they that take such ways to attain the same as he hath taught and appointed by his holy word, in such order, manner, and form as here followeth; ... [those of age but not yet christened must have steadfast faith, true repentance for their sins, 'a full purpose to amend their life' and serve God, and 'must then receive the sacrament of baptism'. As regards infants, their justification 'is wrought by the secret operation of the Holy Ghost in their baptism'. At any time, 'by our own freewill and consenting unto sin', we may lose this 'first justification' and may then recover it only by penance, 'with fasting, alms, prayer' etc.] And here all phantastical imagination, curious reasoning, and vain trust of predestination, is to be laid apart. And according to the plain manner of speaking and teaching of Scripture, in innumerable places, we ought evermore to be in dread of our own frailty and natural pronity to fall to sin, and not to assure ourselves that we be elected. ... (pp. 364-7)

The Article of Good Works

And whereas we speak of good works, it is to be [understood] that we mean not only of outward corporal acts and deeds, but also and rather of all inward spiritual works, motions, and desires, as the love and fear of God, joy in God, godly meditations and thoughts, patience, humility, and such like. And also it is to be [understood] that by good works we mean not the superstitious works of men's own invention, which be not commanded of God, nor approved by his word, in which kind of works many Christian men, and specially of them that were lately called religious (as monks, friars, nuns, and such other), have in times past put their great trust and confidence: . . . we speak of such outward and inward works as God hath prepared for us to walk in, and be done in the faith of Christ. . . . And these works be of two sorts [those done in charity and faith by men 'truly justified', and those 'works of penance' done by sinners in order to recover their justification]. . . . Wherefore as we continue and persevere in good works, so more and more we go forward and proceed in our justification, and in increasing the same. . . . And to ascribe this dignity unto good works, it is no derogation to the grace of God: forasmuch as it is to be confessed that all good works come of the grace of God. And our merits, as St. Augustine saith, be but the gifts of God; and so in ourselves we may not glory. . . . (pp. 370-3)

> *A Necessary Doctrine and Erudition for any Christian Man* (1543), printed in *Formularies of Faith*, ed. Charles Lloyd (1825)

4 Henry VIII's speech to Parliament, December 1545

It was the custom for the Lord Chancellor to answer orations made to the King by the Speaker, but on this occasion the King answered the oration himself, declaring his wish to 'set forth my mind and meaning' plainly and fully. After thanking Parliament for the subsidy they had granted for the wars, for their committal to him of chantries*, etc. (see **VII, 3**), and for their trust in him, he continued as follows.

Yet although I with you, and you with me, be in this perfect love and concord, this friendly amity cannot continue, except both you my Lords temporal, and you my Lords spiritual, and you my loving subjects, study and take pain to amend one thing, which surely is amiss, and far out of order, to the which I most heartily require you, which is, that charity and concord is not amongst you, but discord and dissension beareth rule in every place. St. Paul sayeth to the *Corinthians*, in the 13th chapter, Charity is gentle, Charity is not envious, Charity is not proud and so forth in the said chapter. Behold then what love and charity is amongst you, when the one calleth the other, Heretic and Anabaptist*, and he calleth him again Papist, Hypocrite and Pharisee.

... I must needs judge the ... occasion of this discord, to be partly by negligence of you the fathers and preachers of the spiritualty. ... I see and hear daily that you of the clergy preach one against another, teach one contrary to another, inveigh one against another without charity or discretion. ... Alas, how can the poor souls live in concord when you preachers sow amongst them in your sermons debate and discord. Of you they look for light, and you bring them to darkness. Amend these crimes I exhort you, and set forth God's word, both by true preaching and good example giving, or else I whom God hath appointed his Vicar, and high minister here, will see these divisions extinct, and these enormities corrected, according to my very duty ....

You [also] of the temporalty be not clean and unspotted of malice and envy, for you rail on bishops, speak slanderously of priests, and rebuke and taunt preachers, both contrary to good order and Christian fraternity. If you know surely that a bishop or preacher erreth or teacheth perverse doctrine, come and declare it to some of our Council or to us, to whom is committed by God the high authority to reform and order such causes and behaviours. And be not judges yourselves, of your own phantastical opinions and vain expositions, for in such high causes ye may lightly err. And although you be permitted to read holy Scripture and to have the word of God in your mother tongue, you must understand that it is licensed you so to do, only to inform your own conscience, and to instruct your children and family, and not to dispute and make Scripture a railing and a taunting stock against priests and preachers (as many light persons do). I am very sorry to know and hear, how unreverently that most precious jewel the word of God is disputed, rhymed, sung and jangled in every alehouse and tavern, contrary to the true meaning and doctrine of the same. ...

Therefore, as I said before, be in charity one with another, like brother and brother, love, dread, and serve God (to the which I as your Supreme Head and Sovereign Lord, exhort and require you) and then I doubt not, but that love and league that I spake of in the beginning, shall never be dissolved or broken between us.

Edward Hall, *Henry VIII* (1548), ed. C. Whibley (1904), ii.356-7

5   The Examination of Anne Askew, 1546

On 16 July 1546 Anne Askew, the daughter of a Lincolnshire knight, was burned at Smithfield, together with a Nottinghamshire gentleman John Lascells, an Essex priest, and a tailor. All had been found guilty of denying transubstantiation*, but the attempts of Wriothesley and Rich to make Anne implicate certain noblewomen proved unsuccessful.

The Reformer John Bale, exiled in Germany, wrote a few months later about the 'examinations [of] this faithful witness and holy martyr of God, Anne Askew', saying that he had received information 'in copy by certain Dutch merchants' present at the burnings. He interpolated Anne Askew's own reported utterances with his own characteristically savage comments. Bale's work was subsequently used by Foxe.

The sum of the condemnation of me, Anne Askew, at Guildhall:

They said to me there, that I was an heretic, and condemned by the law, if I would stand in my opinion. I answered that I was no heretic, neither yet deserved I any death by the law of God: but as concerning the faith which I uttered and wrote to the Council, I would not, I said, deny it, because I knew it true. Then would they needs know if I would deny the sacrament to be Christ's body and blood. I said, Yea, for the same Son of God that was born of the Virgin Mary, is now glorious in heaven, and will come again from thence, at the latter day, like as he went up, *Acts* i. And as for that ye call your God, is but a piece of bread. For a more proof thereof (mark it when ye list) let it lie in the box but three months, and it will be mould, and so turn to nothing that is good. Whereupon I am persuaded that it cannot be God.

John Bale:

Christ Jesus, the eternal son of God, was condemned . . . for a seditious heretic, a breaker of their sabbath, a subverter of their people, a defiler of their laws, and a destroyer of their temple, or holy church, *John* vii; *Luke* xxiii; *Matthew* xxvi; *Mark* xiv; and suffered death for it, at their procurement, by the law then used. Is it, then, any marvel if his inferior subject here, and faithful member, do the same, at the cruel calling on and violent vengeance of their posterity? No, no; the servant must follow her master. . . .

But how that dry and corruptible cake [communion-wafer] of theirs should become a god, many men wonder now-a-days, in the light of the gospel, like as they have done aforetime also; and specially, why the wine should not be accepted and set up for a god also, so well as the bread, considering that Christ made so much of the one as of the other. . . . (pp. 212-3)

Anne Askew:
Master Rich [Sir Richard Rich] sent me to the Tower. . . . Then came Rich and one of the Council, charging me, upon my obedience, to shew unto them if I knew man or woman of my sect. My answer was that I knew none. Then they asked me of my lady of Suffolk, my lady of Sussex, my lady of Hertford, my lady Denny, and my lady Fitz-williams. I said, that if I should pronounce anything against them, I were not able to prove it.

John Bale:
. . . How greedily seek you the slaughter of God's true servants, ye blood-thirsty wolves, as the Holy Ghost doth call you, *Psalms* xxv! If the virtuous ladies and most noble women, whose lives ye seek in your mad raging fury . . . have thrown off their shoulders, for 'Christ's easy and gentle burden' (*Matthew* xi), the pope's uneasy and importable yoke (*Luke* xi), happy are they that ever they were born; for thereby have they procured a great quiet and health to their souls. (p. 220)

Anne Askew:
Then they said, there were of the Council that did maintain me. And I said, no. Then they did put me on the rack, because I confessed no ladies or gentlewomen to be of my opinion; and thereon they kept me a long time: and because I lay still, and did not cry, my Lord Chancellor [Sir Thomas Wriothesley] and Master Rich took pains to wrack me in their own hands, till I was nigh dead. (p. 224)

John Bale, *Select Works*, ed. H. Christmas
(*Parker Society*, 1849)

VII

THE PROTESTANT
REVOLUTION

1   Act against Revilers, and for Receiving in Both Kinds, 1547 (1 Edw. VI, c. 1)

The inclusion in the same Act of (a) penalties against irreverent speech on the sacrament of the altar and (b) the introduction of communion in both kinds (see **VI, 1**) was ingenious, since in the circumstances religious conservatives would have found it difficult to vote against the Act as a whole.

In the same Parliament an Act was passed (1 Edw. VI, c. 12) in which several statutes 'in any wise concerning religion or opinions' were repealed (see **Introduction**, pp. 9–10). In addition it was enacted (I Edw. VI, c. 2) that henceforth bishops were to be appointed by letters patent, the electoral procedure laid down in the Act 25 Hen. VIII, c. 20 (**III, 6**) being abandoned. This measure, though in the event short-lived, shows erastian* theory in its most advanced form.

The King's most excellent Majesty, minding the governance and order of his most loving subjects to be in most perfect unity and concord in all things, and in especial in the true faith and religion of God, and wishing the same to be brought to pass with all clemency and mercy on his Highness's part towards them, as his most princely serenity and Majesty hath already declared by evident proofs, to the intent that his most loving subjects, provoked by clemency and goodness of their Prince and King, shall study, rather for love than for fear, to do their duties, first to Almighty God, and then to his Highness and the commonwealth, nourishing concord and love amongst themselves; yet considereth and perceiveth that in a multitude all be not on that sort, that reason and the knowledge of their duties can move them from offence, but many which had need have some bridle of fear, and that the same be men most contentious and arrogant for the most part, or else most blind and ignorant: by the means of which sort of men, many things well and godly instituted and to the edification of many, be perverted and abused, and turned to their own and others' great loss and hindrance, and sometime to extreme destruction, the which doth appear in nothing more or sooner than in matters of religion, and in the great and high mysteries thereof, as in the most comfortable sacrament of the body and blood of our Saviour Jesus Christ, commonly called the sacrament of the altar, and, in Scripture, the supper and table of the Lord, the communion and partaking of the body and blood of Christ; which sacrament was instituted of no less author than of our Saviour, both God and man, when, at his last supper, amongst his Apostles, he did take the bread into his holy hands, and did say: 'Take you and eat, this is my body, which is given and broken for you.' And taking up the chalice or cup, did give thanks, and say: 'This is my blood of the New Testament, which is shed for you, and for many, for the remission of sins,' that whensoever we should do the same, we should do it in the remembrance of him, and to declare and set forth his death and most glorious passion, until his coming. Of the which bread whosoever eateth, or of the which cup whosoever drinketh, unworthily, eateth and drinketh condemnation and judgment to himself, making no difference of the Lord's body; the institution of which sacrament being ordained by Christ, as is beforesaid, and the said words spoken of it here before rehearsed being of eternal, infallible, and undoubted truth; yet the said sacrament (all this notwithstanding) hath been of late marvellously abused by such manner of men before rehearsed, who of wickedness, or else of ignorance and want of learning, for certain abuses heretofore committed of some, in misusing thereof, have condemned in their hearts and speech the whole thing, and contemptuously depraved, despised, or reviled the same most holy and blessed sacrament, and not only disputed and reasoned unreverently and ungodly of that most high mystery, but also, in their sermons, preachings, readings, lectures, communications, arguments, talks, rhymes, songs, plays, or jests, name or call it by such vile and unseemly words as Christian ears do abhor to hear rehearsed.

For reformation whereof, be it enacted ... that whatsoever person or persons from and after the first day of May next coming, shall deprave, despise, or contemn the said most blessed sacrament, in contempt thereof, by any contemptuous words, or by any words of depraving, despising, or reviling, or ... shall advisedly, in any other wise, contemn, despise, or revile the said most blessed sacrament, contrary to the effects and declaration abovesaid; that then he or they shall suffer imprisonment of his or their bodies, and make fine and ransom at the King's will and pleasure.

[II-V Justices of the peace are to have 'full power and authority' to take information of offenders, who shall be tried at quarter sessions. The bishop of the particular diocese (or his deputy) is to be present at the trial.]

*   *   *

VIII   And forasmuch as it is more agreeable, both to the first institution of the said sacrament of the most precious body and blood of our Saviour Jesus Christ, and also more conformable to the common use and practice both of the Apostles and of the primitive Church, by the space of 500 years and more after Christ's ascension, that the said blessed sacrament should be ministered to all Christian people under both the kinds of bread and wine, than under the form of bread only, and also it is more agreeable to the first institution of Christ, and to the usage of the Apostles and the primitive Church, that the people being present should receive the same with the priest, than that the priest should receive it alone; therefore be it enacted ... that the said most blessed sacrament be hereafter commonly delivered and ministered unto the people within this Church of England and Ireland and other the King's dominions, under both the kinds, that is to say, of bread and wine, except necessity otherwise require: and also that the priest which shall minister the same, shall, at the least one day before, exhort all persons which shall be present likewise to resort and prepare themselves to receive the same.

And when the day prefixed cometh, after a godly exhortation by the minister made (wherein shall be further expressed the benefit and comfort promised to them which worthily receive the said holy sacrament, and [the] danger and indignation of God threatened to them which shall presume to receive the same unworthily, to the end that every man may try and examine his own conscience before he shall receive the same), the said minister shall not, without lawful cause, deny the same to any person that will devoutly and humbly desire it; any law, statute, ordinance, or custom contrary thereunto in any wise notwithstanding; not condemning hereby the usage of any Church out of the King's Majesty's dominions.

Stat. Realm, iv.2-3

2   Religious Disputes in Southern England

Thomas Hancock, from whose autobiography these passages are drawn, graduated B.A. at Oxford in 1532 and subsequently became curate at Amport in his
native county Hampshire. In 1546 he had been suspended for attacking the
sacrificial character of the mass. After the accession of Edward VI he preached
so aggressively against transubstantiation* as to offend religious conservatives
and even to risk contravening the 'Act against Revilers' (1 above).

The first year of the reign of King Edward VI, I the said Thomas,
having licence of Bishop Cranmer, preached at Christchurch Twinham
[Hampshire] where I was born, Mr. Smythe, vicar of Christchurch and
bachelor of divinity being present; where I, taking my place out of the
16 *St. John*, v. 8, [said]. . . . Here doth our Saviour Christ say that he
goeth to the Father and that we shall see him no more. The priest being
then at mass, I declared unto the people that [what] the priest doth
hold over his head [the consecrated bread and wine] they did see with
their bodily eyes, but our Saviour Christ doth here say plainly that we
shall see him no more. Then you that do kneel unto it, pray unto it
and honour it as God, do make an idol of it, and yourselves do commit
most horrible idolatry. Whereat the said vicar, Mr. Smythe, sitting in
his chair in the face of the pulpit, spake these words, 'Mr. Hancock,
you have done well until now and now have you played an ill cow's
part, which when she hath given a good mess of milk, overthroweth
all with her foot, and so all is lost', and with these words he got him
out of the church. . . .

[When Hancock preached similarly at Salisbury, the Mayor would
have jailed him, had not several of his substantial local backers, headed
by a woollen-draper named Harry Dymoke, offered to stand surety
for him. The Lord Chief Justice then charged him with causing an
uproar, and forced him to find ten sureties of £10 each, and to sign a
recognisance of £90 for his future conformity to the law. Hancock
resolved to appeal to the Protector.]

This done, I rode from Salisbury unto my Lord of Somerset his Grace,
who lay at that time at Syon. I requested his Grace that I might have
his letter for the discharge of them that were bound for me: he caused
my Lord Treasurer his honour that now is, who then was Master of
the Requests [William Cecil] to write to my Lord Chief Justice for

the discharge of the bond. Which letter, whilst I was with my Lord [Chief Justice] at Hampton [Southampton] to deliver, the bell rang to the sermon. My Lord asked me whether I minded to preach. I answered yea. My Lord said unto me that Hampton was a haven town, and that if I should teach such doctrine as I taught at Sarum [Salisbury], the town would be divided, and so should it be a way or a gap for the enemy to enter in; and therefore he commanded me that I should not preach there. I answered that I would not take that for a forbidding, but that forsomuch as the people resorted to the church at the ringing of the bell to hear the word of God, they should not return home again void of God's word. My Lord said again unto me that I should not preach, and that there was one in the Tower (meaning Bishop Gardiner) that he would believe before 400 such as I was. I answered him that he spake those words betwixt him and me, but if I had record of them, he would not speak them.

So my Lord sent for the Mayor and his brethren. Mr. Mayor asked me whether I would be content that another should supply the room for me. I answered, yea, and that I was as willing to hear the word as to preach myself. So did Mr. Mayor send to one Mr. Griffith, who did preach; and my Lord being present, he challenged him that he, being Chief Justice of the Law did suffer the images in the church, the idol hanging in a string over the altar [in the vessel known as the pyx], candlesticks and tapers on them upon the altar, and the people honouring the idol, contrary to the law; with much other good doctrine. I praised God for it. And thus were my friends of Sarum that were bound for me discharged their bond.

This trouble being overcome, another followeth, for after this I was called the same year, which was the first year of King Edward, to be the minister of God's word at the town of Poole, in county Dorset, which town was at the time wealthy, for they embraced God's word; they were in favours with the rulers and governors of the realm. They were the first that in that part of England were called Protestants; they did love one another, and every one glad of the company of the others, and so God poured his blessing plentifully upon them; but now I am sorry to set my pen to write it, they have become poor; they have no love to God's word. . . .

I being minister of God's word in that town of Poole, preaching the word upon some Sunday in the month of July, inveighed against idolatry and covetousness, taking my place out of the 6th of *Timothy*. . . .

The brightness of the Godhead is such that it passeth the brightness of the sun, of angels and all creatures, so that it cannot be seen with our bodily eyes, for no man hath seen God at any time and liveth. The priest at that time being at mass, if it be so that no man hath seen God, nor can see God with these bodily eyes, then that which the priest lifteth over his head is not God, for you do see it with your bodily eyes: if it be not God, you may not honour it as God, neither for God. Whereat old Thomas Whyte, a great rich merchant and a ringleader of the papists, rose out of his seat and went out of the church, saying, 'Come from him, good people; he came from the devil and teacheth unto you devilish doctrine.' John Notherel, alias John Spicer, followed him, saying, 'It shall be God when thou shalt be but a knave.' [Hancock describes further clashes with Whyte and his adherents, who threatened to disembowel him in the church and reviled the Mayor of Poole when the latter came to his aid. After the accession of Mary, he was excepted from the Queen's general pardon, and fled with his wife and son to Geneva.]

> Narratives of the Days of the Reformation, ed. J. G. Nichols (Camden Society, old series, lxxvii, 1859), pp. 72–8

3 Act dissolving the Chantries*, etc. 1547 (1 Edw. VI, c. 14)

Chantries, the main institutions covered by the following Act, were foundations providing money for masses to be said regularly for the souls of the founder and any others named by him. An Act of 1545 (37 Hen. VIII, c. 4) had vested chantries, etc., in the hands of the King, and a number of dissolutions had taken place after a survey by commissioners. The stated intention of the 1545 Act had been to obtain money for the wars against France and Scotland. In the following Act, however, specifically Protestant doctrinal reasons are given for the proposed dissolutions. The preamble reflects an attitude very prevalent during Edward's reign: an increased determination to abolish all usages regarded as 'superstitious'. Undoubtedly the government also had financial motives.

Although under the terms of the Act, all 'fraternities, brotherhoods and guilds' were given to the King, general funds of secular guilds were not in fact taken. A charge was levied on these guilds to cover funds previously devoted to 'superstitious' uses.

New surveys were completed by the summer of 1548: see 4 below for examples of both a Henrician and an Edwardian survey. According to Camden's estimate

Chantry lands

(c. 1586) the dissolution involved some 2,374 chantries, 90 colleges and 110 hospitals, i.e. almshouses. The total value of the endowments involved is difficult to estimate but it was small in relation to that of the monasteries, since most chantries had very low incomes. The surveys show that during the 20 years or so before the Dissolution, the incomes, lands and properties of many chantries had already been 'resumed' by patrons and others, possibly in anticipation of government confiscation.

The King's most loving subjects, the Lords spiritual and temporal and the Commons in this present Parliament assembled, considering that a great part of superstition and errors in Christian religion hath been brought into the minds and estimation of men, by reason of the ignorance of their very true and perfect salvation through the death of Jesus Christ, and by devising and phantasing vain opinions of purgatory* and masses satisfactory, to be done for them which be departed, the which doctrine and vain opinion by nothing more is maintained and upholden, than by the abuse of trentals [a set of thirty requiem masses], chantries, and other provisions made for the continuance of the said blindness and ignorance; and further considering and understanding that the alteration, change, and amendment of the same, and converting to good and godly uses; as in erecting of grammar schools to the education of youth in virtue and godliness, the further augmenting of the Universities, and better provision for the poor and needy, cannot, in this present Parliament, be provided and conveniently done, nor cannot ne ought to any other manner person be committed, than to the King's Highness, whose Majesty, with and by the advice of his Highness's most prudent Council, can and will most wisely and beneficially, both for the honour of God and the weal of this his Majesty's realm, order, alter, convert, and dispose the same. And calling further to their remembrance ... [there follows a recital of 37 Hen. VIII, c. 4, for the Dissolution of Chantries, etc.]:

It is now ordained and enacted ... that all manner of colleges, free chapels, and chantries, having been or *in esse* within five years next before the first day of this present Parliament, which were not in actual and real possession of the said late King, nor in the actual and real possession of the King our Sovereign Lord that now is, nor excepted in the said former Act ... and all manors, lands, tenements, rents, tithes*, pensions, portions, and other hereditaments and things above mentioned, belonging to them or any of them ... and also all annual rents, profits, and emoluments, at any time within five years next before the beginning of this present Parliament, employed, paid or

bestowed toward or for the maintenance, supportation, or finding of
any stipendiary priest, intended by any Act or writing to have continuance for ever, shall, by the authority of this present Parliament,
immediately after the feast of Easter next coming, be adjudged and
deemed, and also be, in the very actual and real possession and seisin
of the King our Sovereign Lord, and his heirs and successors for ever,
without any office or other inquisition thereof to be had or found, and
in as large and ample manner and form as the priests, wardens, masters,
ministers, governors, rulers, or other incumbents of them or any of
them . . . had, occupied, or enjoyed, or now hath, occupieth, or enjoy-
eth the same, and as though all and singular the said colleges, free
chapels, chantries, stipends, salaries of priests, and the said manors,
lands . . . and other the premises . . . were in this present Act specially,
particularly and certainly rehearsed, named, and expressed by express
words, names, surnames, corporations, titles, and faculties, and in their
natures, kinds, and qualities.

*   *   *   ·

VII   And furthermore be it ordained and enacted . . . that the King
our Sovereign Lord shall, from the said feast of Easter next coming,
have and enjoy to him, his heirs and successors for ever, all fraternities,
brotherhoods and guilds, being within the realm of England and Wales
and other the King's dominions; and all manors, lands, tenements, and
other hereditaments belonging to them or any of them . . . and shall
by virtue of this Act be judged and deemed in actual and real possession of our said Sovereign Lord the King, his heirs and successors,
from the said feast of Easter next coming, for ever, without any inquisition or office thereof to be had or found.

[VIII-XII   The King may appoint commissioners with power to
survey the properties covered by this Act. The commissioners are also
empowered to assign lands for the support of a schoolmaster or preacher,
where the keeping of a grammar school or preaching was required by
the original foundation; to endow vicars sufficiently in cases where the
parish church is a foundation which will come into the King's hands
under the terms of the Act; to assign chantry lands for the maintenance
of additional priests where necessary; to make 'rules concerning the
service, user, and demeanour' of priests and schoolmasters appointed
by them; and to assign pensions to the priests of dissolved chantries and
to poor persons hitherto dependent on them for 'yearly relief'.]

XIII   And also be it ordained and enacted . . . that our Sovereign Lord the King shall have and enjoy all such goods, chattels, jewels, plate, ornaments, and other moveables, as were, or be, the common goods of every such college, chantry, free chapel, or stipendiary priest, belonging or annexed to the furniture or service of their several foundations, or abused of any of the said corporations in the abuses aforesaid, the property whereof was not altered nor changed before the eighth day of December in the year of our Lord God 1547.

*   *   *

[XV   The Act shall not extend to colleges, hostels and halls at the Universities of Oxford and Cambridge, nor to the Colleges of Winchester and Eton, nor to 'any chapel made . . . for the ease of the people dwelling distant from the parish church'. A few other exceptions are made.]

*   *   *

[XIX   Lands, etc. 'appointed to the King by this Act' are to be in the survey of the Court of Augmentations (see V, 3), except (XXXI) those within the Duchy of Lancaster.]

*   *   *

Stat. Realm, iv.24-33

4   (a) and (b) The Chantry* Surveys

In each county a body of commissioners surveyed the many foundations affected by the Chantry Acts. The following two extracts concern the same chantry at Topcliffe, North Yorkshire. They afford a comparison between the Henrician survey, mainly concerned with the endowments, and the Edwardian survey, which supplemented this information by enquiry into the character, learning and usefulness of each incumbent.

THE CHANTRY OF OUR LADY, IN THE PARISH CHURCH OF TOPCLIFFE, YORKSHIRE
[(a) HENRICIAN CERTIFICATE, 1546]

Davye Bele incumbent. The same chantry is of the foundation of Richard Grome and Thomas Allanson, to say mass and other divine service, and to pray for the founders' souls and all Christian souls, and to help the curate in the choir of the same church, as by foundation, dated the Monday next after the feast of St. Michael the Archangel, the 15th year of the reign of King Henry VII, and a feoffment made to certain persons by the said founders of certain lands contained in the rental, for the sustentation of the incumbent there.

The same chantry is within the said parish church and the necessity is as afore is mentioned, and to help the curate to minister to the parochians, being many in number. There is no lands sold ne alienated since the 4th day of February *anno regni regis Henrici VIII*, 27 [1546].

Goods, ornaments and plate pertaining to the said chantry, as appeareth by inventory: goods, nil; plate, nil. First certain lands and tenements in the tenure of divers persons lying in sundry places, viz: of Marget Daget, 58s. lying in Catton; James Tyrrye, 12s. 1d.; John Dunne, 3s. 4½d. and Leonard Bell, 8s., lying in Dalton; and Thomas Wyghte, 15s., lying in Crakhall. In all, £4 16s. 5½d. Whereof, payable to the King's Majesty for haver silver, 2s. 4d.; to the Cathedral Church of York, 2s.; to William Staveley, 1½d.; and for the Tenths [see **III, 9**], 6s. 8d. In all, 11s. 1½d. And so remaineth £4 6s. 4d.

[(b) EDWARDIAN CERTIFICATE, 1548]

David Bell, incumbent there, of the age of 48 years, of good conversation and qualities, and mean [medium] learning, having a yearly stipend of 106s. 8d. of the King's Majesty, over and besides his said chantry. Also there is within the said parish six chantry and stipendiary priests, besides the vicar, whose names do appear [in other entries]. And there is belonging to the said parish of houseling people [communicants] to the number of 960. And there is no lands ne tenements wasted ne sold since [27 Nov. 1545]. The yearly value of the said chantry, as shall appear by the particulars of the same, £4 16s. 4d. In resolutes [payments] yearly going forth of the same 6s. 8d. And so remaineth clear, £4 9s. 8d. Goods, . . . plate, nil.

Yorkshire Chantry Surveys, ed. W. Page (*Surtees Society*, xci, pt. I, 1894), pp. 86–7; (xcii, pt. II, 1895), pp. 478–9

5 The First Edwardian Act of Uniformity, 1549 (2 & 3 Edw. VI, c. 1)

See **Introduction**, pp. 10-11. Although the first sentence of this Act refers to 'divers forms of common prayer', the differences between the various medieval Uses were in fact comparatively small. The Act established as the only legal form of worship from Whitsunday 1549 the First English Prayer Book. In 1550 a further Act (3 & 4 Edw. VI, c. 10) ordered that all old service books should be given up to be destroyed.

Where of long time there hath been had in this realm of England and in Wales divers forms of common prayer, commonly called the service of the Church; that is to say the Use of Sarum, of York, of Bangor, and of Lincoln; and besides the same now of late much more divers and sundry forms and fashions have been used in the cathedral and parish churches of England and Wales, as well concerning the Matins or Morning Prayer and the Evensong, as also concerning the Holy Communion, commonly called the Mass, with divers and sundry rites and ceremonies concerning the same, and in the administration of other sacraments of the Church: and as the doers and executors of the said rites and ceremonies, in other form than of late years they have been used, were pleased therewith, so other, not using the same rites and ceremonies, were thereby greatly offended. And albeit the King's Majesty, with the advice of his most entirely beloved uncle the Lord Protector and other of his Highness's Council, hath heretofore divers times essayed to stay innovations or new rites concerning the premises; yet the same hath not had such good success as his Highness required in that behalf:

Whereupon his Highness by the most prudent advice aforesaid, being pleased to bear with the frailty and weakness of his subjects in that behalf, of his great clemency hath not been only content to abstain from punishment of those that have offended in that behalf, for that his Highness taketh that they did it of a good zeal; but also to the intent a uniform quiet and godly order should be had concerning the premises, hath appointed the Archbishop of Canterbury, and certain of the most learned and discreet bishops, and other learned men of this realm, to consider and ponder the premises; and thereupon having as well eye and respect to the most sincere and pure Christian religion taught by the Scripture, as to the usages in the primitive Church, should draw and make one convenient and meet order, rite and fashion of common and open prayer and administration of the sacraments, to be had and used in his Majesty's realm of England and in Wales; the which at this time, by the aid of the Holy Ghost, with one uniform agreement is of them concluded, set forth, and delivered to his Highness, to his great comfort and quietness of mind, in a book entitled, The Book of the Common Prayer and Administration of the Sacraments, and other Rites and Ceremonies of the Church, after the use of the Church of England.

Wherefore the Lords spiritual and temporal and the Commons in this present Parliament assembled, considering as well the most godly travail of the King's Highness, of the Lord Protector, and other of his Highness's Council, in gathering and collecting the said Archbishop, bishops, and learned men together, as the godly prayers, orders, rites, and ceremonies in the said book mentioned, and the considerations of altering those things which be altered, and retaining those things which be retained in the said book, but also the honour of God and great quietness, which by the grace of God shall ensue upon the one and uniform rite and order in such common prayer and rites and external ceremonies to be used throughout England and in Wales, at Calais and the marches of the same, do give to his Highness most hearty and lowly thanks for the same; and humbly pray, that it may be ordained and enacted by his Majesty, with the assent of the Lords and Commons in this present Parliament assembled, and by authority of the same, that all and singular person and persons that have offended concerning the premises, other than such person and persons as now be and remain in ward in the Tower of London, or in the Fleet, may be pardoned thereof; and that all and singular ministers in any cathedral or parish church or other place within this realm of England, Wales, Calais, and the marches of the same, or other the King's dominions, shall, from and after the feast of Pentecost next coming, be bound to say and use the Matins, Evensong, celebration of the Lord's Supper, commonly called the Mass, and administration of each of the sacraments, and all their common and open prayer, in such order and form as is mentioned in the said book, and none other or otherwise.

II   And albeit that the same be so godly and good, that they give occasion to every honest and conformable man most willingly to embrace them, yet lest any obstinate person who willingly would disturb so godly order and quiet in this realm should not go unpunished, that it may also be ordained and enacted . . . that if any manner of parson, vicar, or other whatsoever minister, that ought or should sing or say common prayer mentioned in the said book, or minister the sacraments, shall after the said feast of Pentecost next coming refuse to use the said common prayers, or to minister the sacraments in such cathedral or parish church or other places as he should use or minister the same, in such order and form as they be mentioned and set forth in the said book; or shall use, wilfully and obstinately standing in the same, any other rite, ceremony, order, form, or manner of Mass openly or privily, or Matins, Evensong, administration of the sacraments, or other open prayer than is mentioned and set forth in the said book (open prayer in and throughout this Act, is meant that prayer which is for other to come unto or hear, either in common churches or private chapels or oratories, commonly called the service of the Church); or shall preach, declare, or speak anything in the derogation or depraving of the said book, or anything therein contained, or of any part thereof, and shall be thereof lawfully convicted according to the laws of this realm, by verdict of twelve men, or by his own confession, or by the notorious evidence of the facts, shall lose and forfeit to the King's Highness, his heirs and successors, for his first offence, the profit of such one of his spiritual benefices or promotions as it shall please the King's Highness to assign or appoint, coming and arising in one whole year next after his conviction; and also that the same person so convicted shall for the same offence suffer imprisonment by the space of six months, without bail . . . [for a second offence he shall suffer imprisonment for one year, and be deprived of all spiritual promotions, and for a third offence, suffer life imprisonment. Unbeneficed persons shall suffer six months imprisonment for a first offence, and life imprisonment for a second].

III   And it is ordained and enacted . . . that if any person or persons whatsoever, after the said feast of Pentecost next coming, shall in any interludes, plays, songs, rhymes, or by other open words declare or speak anything in the derogation, depraving, or despising of the same book or of anything therein contained, or any part thereof, or shall by open fact, deed, or by open threatenings, compel or cause, or otherwise procure or maintain any parson, vicar, or other minister in any cathedral or parish church, or in any chapel or other place, to sing or say any common and open prayer, or to minister any sacrament otherwise or in any other manner or form than is mentioned in the said book; or that by any of the said means shall unlawfully interrupt or let [hinder] any parson, vicar or other ministers in any cathedral or parish church, chapel, or any other place, to sing or say common and open prayer, or to minister the sacraments, or any of them, in any such manner and form as is mentioned in the said book; [then he shall be fined £10 (or suffer three months imprisonment for default in payment) for the first offence, £20 (or six months imprisonment) for a second, and forfeiture of all goods and life imprisonment for a third].

*   *   *

VI Provided always, that it shall be lawful to any man that understandeth the Greek, Latin, and Hebrew tongue, or other strange tongue, to say and have the said prayers, heretofore specified, of Matins and Evensong in Latin, or any such other tongue, saying the same privately, as they do understand.

And for the further encouraging of learning in the tongues in the Universities of Cambridge and Oxford, to use and exercise in their common and open prayer in their chapels, being no parish churches or other places of prayer, the Matins, Evensong, Litany, and all other prayers (the Holy Communion, commonly called the Mass, excepted) prescribed in the said book, in Greek, Latin, or Hebrew, anything in this present Act to the contrary notwithstanding.

*   *   *

VIII Provided also ... that the books concerning the said services shall at the costs and charges of the parishioners of every parish and cathedral church be attained and gotten before the feast of Pentecost next following, or before; and that all such parish and cathedral churches ... shall within three weeks next after the said books so attained and gotten use the said service. ...

*   *   *

Stat. Realm, iv.37–9

6 Act to take away all positive Laws against Marriage of Priests, 1549 (2 & 3 Edw. VI, c. 21)

Although both Convocation and Commons had agreed in 1547 to measures sanctioning the marriage of priests, opposition in the Lords delayed the passing of this Statute until February 1549. See **VIII, 2** for the action taken against the many priests who married during the four years which elapsed between the enactment of this Statute and its repeal in the first year of Mary's reign.

Although it were not only better for the estimation of priests and other ministers in the Church of God, to live chaste, sole, and separate from the company of women and the bond of marriage, but also thereby they might the better intend to the administration of the gospel, and be less intricated and troubled with the charge of household, being free and unburdened from the care and cost of finding wife and children, and that it were most to be wished that they would willingly and of their selves endeavour themselves to a perpetual chastity and abstinence from the use of women:

Yet forasmuch as the contrary hath rather been seen, and such uncleanness of living, and other great inconveniences, not meet to be rehearsed, have followed of compelled chastity, and of such laws as have prohibited those (such persons) the godly use of marriage; it were better and rather to be suffered in the commonwealth, that those which could not contain, should, after the counsel of Scripture, live in holy marriage, than feignedly abuse with worse enormity outward chastity or single life.

Be it therefore enacted ... that all and every law and laws positive, canons, constitutions, and ordinances heretofore made by the authority of man only, which doth prohibit or forbid marriage to any ecclesiastical or spiritual person or persons, of what estate, condition, or degree they be, or by what name or names soever they be called, which by God's law may lawfully marry, in all and every article, branch and sentence, concerning only the prohibition for the marriage of the persons aforesaid, shall be utterly void and of none effect; and that all manner of forfeitures, pains, penalties, crimes, or actions which were in the said laws contained, and the same did follow, concerning the prohibition for the marriage of the persons aforesaid, be clearly and utterly void, frustrate, and of none effect, to all intents, constructions, and purposes, as well concerning marriages heretofore made by any of the ecclesiastical or spiritual persons aforesaid, as also such which hereafter shall be duly and lawfully had, celebrate, and made, betwixt the persons which by the laws of God may lawfully marry.

II   Provided always, and be it enacted ... that this Act, or anything therein contained, shall not extend to give any liberty to any person to marry without asking in the church, or without any other ceremony being appointed by the order prescribed and set forth in the book entitled The Book of Common Prayer and the Administration of the Sacraments, anything above mentioned to the contrary in any wise notwithstanding.

*   *   *

Stat. Realm, iv.67

7   The Second Edwardian Act of Uniformity, 1552 (5 & 6 Edw. VI, c. 1)

See **Introduction**, p. 11. Unlike the first Edwardian Act of Uniformity, this Act enjoins attendance at common prayer every Sunday 'upon pain of punishment by the censures of the Church'.

The reference in § IV to the 'form and manner of making and consecrating archbishops, bishops, priests, and deacons' is to Cranmer's *Ordinal* (first published 1550, and now revised), in which the orders were restricted to those of bishop, priest and deacon, and the medieval ceremonies of ordination and consecration amended to some extent. (See also **VIII, 2**.)

Where there hath been a very godly order set forth by authority of Parliament, for common prayer and administration of the sacraments, to be used in the mother tongue within the Church of England, agreeable to the word of God and the primitive Church, very comfortable to all good people desiring to live in Christian conversation, and most profitable to the estate of this realm, upon the which the mercy, favour, and blessing of Almighty God is in no wise so readily and plenteously poured as by common prayers, due using of the sacraments, and often preaching of [the] gospel with the devotion of the hearers:

And yet this notwithstanding, a great number of people in divers parts of this realm, following their own sensuality and living either without knowledge or due fear of God, do wilfully and damnably before Almighty God abstain and refuse to come to their parish churches and other places where common prayer, administration of the sacraments, and preaching of the word of God is used upon the Sundays and other days ordained to be holy-days.

For reformation hereof, be it enacted ... that from and after the feast of All Saints next coming [1 November, 1552], all and every person and persons inhabiting within this realm, or any other the King's Majesty's dominions, shall diligently and faithfully, having no lawful or reasonable excuse to be absent, endeavour themselves to resort to their parish church or chapel accustomed, or upon reasonable let [hindrance] thereof, to some usual place where common prayer and such service of God shall be used in such time of let, upon every Sunday, and other days ordained and used to be kept as holy-days, and then and there to abide orderly and soberly during the time of the common prayer, preachings, or other service of God there to be used and ministered, upon pain of punishment by the censures of the Church.

II   And for the due execution hereof, the King's most excellent Majesty, the Lords temporal and all the Commons in this present [Parliament] assembled, doeth in God's name earnestly require and charge all the archbishops, bishops, and other ordinaries*, that they shall endeavour themselves to the uttermost of their knowledge, that the due and true execution hereof may be had throughout their dioceses and charges, as they will answer before God for such evils and plagues wherewith Almighty God may justly punish his people for neglecting this good and wholesome law.

III   And for their authority in this behalf, be it further likewise enacted ... that all and singular the same archbishops, bishops, and all other their officers exercising ecclesiastical jurisdiction ... within their dioceses, shall have full power and authority by this Act to reform, correct, and punish by censures of the Church, all and singular persons which shall offend, within any their jurisdictions or dioceses, after the said feast of All Saints next coming against this Act and Statute; any other law, statute, privilege, liberty, or provision heretofore made, had, or suffered to the contrary notwithstanding.

IV   And because there hath arisen in the use and exercise of the aforesaid common service in the Church, heretofore set forth, divers doubts for the fashion and manner of the ministration of same, rather by the curiosity of the minister, and mistakers, than of any other worthy cause:

Therefore, as well for the more plain and manifest explanation hereof, as for the more perfection of the said order of common service, in some places where it is necessary to make the same prayers and fashion of service more earnest and fit to stir Christian people to the true honouring of Almighty God, the King's most excellent Majesty, with the assent of the Lords and Commons in this present Parliament assembled, and by the authority of the same, hath caused the foresaid order of common service, entitled The Book of Common Prayer, to be faithfully and godly perused, explained, and made fully perfect, and by the foresaid authority hath annexed and joined it, so explained and perfected, to this present Statute: adding also a form and manner of making and consecrating archbishops, bishops, priests, and deacons, to be of like force, authority, and value as the same like aforesaid book, entitled, The Book of Common Prayer, was before, and to be accepted, received, used, and esteemed in like sort and manner, and with the same clauses of provisions and exceptions, to all intents, constructions, and purposes, as by the Act of Parliament made in the second year of the King's Majesty's reign [5 above] was ordained and limited, expressed and appointed for the uniformity of service and administration of the sacraments throughout the realm, upon such several pains as in the said Act of Parliament is expressed.

And the said former Act to stand in full force, and strength, to all intents and constructions, and to be applied ... to and for the establishing of the Book of Common Prayer, now explained and hereunto annexed, and also the said form of making of archbishops, bishops, priests, and deacons hereunto annexed as it was for the former book.

V   And by the authority aforesaid it is now further enacted, that if any manner of person or persons inhabiting and being within this realm, or any other the King's Majesty's dominions, shall after the said feast of All Saints willingly and wittingly hear and be present at any other manner or form of common prayer, of administration of the sacraments, of making of ministers in the churches, or of any other rites contained in the book annexed to this Act, than is mentioned and set forth in the said book, or that is contrary to the form of sundry provisions and exceptions contained in the foresaid former Statute, and shall be thereof convicted according to the laws of this realm, before the justices of assize, justices of *oyer* and *terminer*, justices of peace in their sessions, or any of them, by the verdict of twelve men, or by his or their own confession or otherwise, shall for the first offence suffer imprisonment for six months, without bail ... and for the second offence ... imprisonment for one whole year; and for the third offence ... imprisonment during his or their lives.

VI And for the more knowledge to be given hereof, and better observation of this law, be it enacted . . . that all and singular curates shall upon one Sunday every quarter of the year during one whole year next following the foresaid feast of All Saints next coming, read this present Act in the church at the time of the most assembly, and likewise once in every year following; at the same time declaring unto the people, by the authority of the Scripture, how the mercy and goodness of God hath in all ages been showed to his people in their necessities and extremities, by means of hearty and faithful prayers made to Almighty God, especially where people be gathered together with one faith and mind, to offer up their hearts by prayer, as the best sacrifices that Christian men can yield.

Stat. Realm, iv.130-1

collective prayer

8   Robert Parkyn's Narrative of the Reformation

Robert Parkyn became curate of Adwick-le-Street near Doncaster in the early 1540s and remained in this living throughout all the religious changes which occurred until his death in 1569. Unlike the majority of the parochial clergy, he was comparatively well-educated, possessed private means and a large library, and wrote numerous works: his narrative of the Reformation, from which the following extracts are drawn, was written in the reign of Mary. In 2 above we read the forcibly-expressed views of a thorough-going Protestant radical of the mid-century, Thomas Hancock. Below we have, from Parkyn, an equally vigorous exposition, but from the very opposite standpoint: that of a conservative, late-medieval Catholic, deeply and sincerely committed to the centuries-old traditional ways. He had a great regard for medieval (especially mystical) writings, and for old legends e.g. about the Virgin Mary, whether these were substantiated by Scriptural texts or not. In his narrative he seems much less concerned with the rejection of the pope's authority than with changes in old-established doctrines and rites. It would also appear that the revolutionary changes ordered by the government were usually complied with, at all events in Parkyn's own deanery.

The fact that Parkyn remained in his living throughout all the religious changes, conforming with the Elizabethan Settlement only a few years after expressing the sentiments below, illustrates the generally submissive nature of the Tudor parochial clergy. Many, unlike Parkyn, were ill-educated and poor and life was by no means easy for them: their rather bewildered acquiescence in all the changes can hardly remain a matter for censure four hundred years later.

40° table wise rather than altar wise

Be it known to all men to whom this present writing shall come, see, hear or read, that in the year of our Lord God 1532 and in the twenty-fourth year of the reign of King Henry VIII these grievous matters ensuing first began to take root; and after by process of time was accomplished and brought to pass in very deed within this realm of England, to the great discomfort of all such as was true Christians. . . .

[Parkyn narrates very briefly, and often inaccurately, the events of Henry's reign, condemning the 'counsel of one wretch and heretic Thomas Cromwell and such other of his affinity'. He then goes on to speak in highly critical detail of all the various stages of the Edwardian Reformation. In addition to the criticisms given below, he condemns the confiscation of ecclesiastical properties; the abrogation of many old ceremonies (e.g. the bearing of palms on Palm Sunday, Rogation Day processions, etc.) and of traditional doctrines such as purgatory*; the order to remove 'all images, pictures, tables, crucifixes, tabernacles' from churches, etc.]

And so [by the First Edwardian Act of Uniformity, 1549 (2 & 3 Edw. VI, c. 1) – 5 above] the holy mass was utterly deposed throughout all this realm of England and other the King's dominions at the said Pentecost, and in place thereof a communion to be said in English without any elevation of Christ's body and blood under form of bread and wine, or adoration. . . .

But in the first week of November [by the Second Edwardian Act of Uniformity, 1552 (5 & 6 Edw. VI, c. 1) – 7 above] the . . . book (called the Book of Common Prayer) came forth . . . wherein many things was altered from the other English book before used, for the table (whereat the Holy Communion was ministered in the choir) was had down into the body of the church in many places, and set in the mid aisle among the people, the ends whereof stood east and west, and the priest on the north side, his face turned toward the south . . . [saying] to every one of them [partaking in the Communion], 'Take and eat this in remembrance that Christ died for thee, and feed of [should be 'on'] him in thy heart by faith with thanksgiving'. That done, the priest . . . did give unto them also the chalice or cup . . . saying, 'Drink this in remembrance that Christ's blood was shed for thee and be thankful', straightly forbidding that any adoration should be done thereunto, for that were idolatry (said the book) and to be abhorred of all faithful Christians. And as concerning the natural body and blood of Our

Saviour Jesus Christ (said the book also) they are in heaven and not here in earth, for it were against the truth of Christ's true natural body to be in more places than in one at one time. [An almost verbatim reference to part of the Black Rubric: see **Introduction**, p. 11.] Oh, how abominable heresy and unseeming order was this, let every man ponder in his own conscience. . . .

[After speaking of the great rejoicing in the north when Mary was proclaimed Queen, Parkyn continues:]

But all such as were of heretical opinions, with bishops and priests having wives, did nothing rejoice, but began to be ashamed of themselves, for the common people would point them with fingers in places when they saw them. . . .

Thus through grace of the Holy Ghost the strait of holy Church something began to amend and to arise from the old heresies before used in this realm. . . .

And so to proceed further . . . a great parliament [was] holden at Westminster [November 1554 – January 1555] wherein all such Acts was utterly abolished . . . as had been made aforetime against the pope of Rome, and he to have from that time as high authority and jurisdiction within this realm . . . as ever had any of his predecessors [Mary's Second Statute of Repeal, 1554 (1 & 2 Philip & Mary, c. 8) – **VIII, 4**.] . . . Then began holy Church to rejoice in God, singing both with heart and tongue *Te Deum Laudamus*, but heretical persons (as there was many) rejoiced nothing thereat. Oh, it was joy to hear and see how these carnal priests (which had led their lives in fornication with their whores and harlots) did lour and look down, when they were commanded to leave and forsake the concubines and harlots and to do open penance according to the Canon Law [See **VIII, 2**]. . . . So to be brief, all old ceremonies laudably used beforetime in the holy Church was then revived, daily frequented and used. . . .

'Robert Parkyn's Narrative of the Reformation', ed. A. G. Dickens, *English Historical Review*, lxii (1947), pp. 58-83

VIII

THE MARIAN REACTION

1 Mary's First Statute of Repeal, 1553 (1 Mary, Stat. 2, c. 2)

Shortly after her accession in July 1553, Mary issued a Proclamation in which she made clear her wish that her subjects should be of that religion which 'she hath ever professed from her infancy'. Nevertheless, religious compulsion would not be used at present, until 'further order may be taken'. Strife and contention were forbidden however, and also any unlicensed preaching or printing about the Scriptures. She enjoined all her subjects to 'live together in quiet sort and Christian charity'.

Mary's first Parliament met during the last three months of 1553. The following Act restored the situation which had obtained in the last year (1546-7) of Henry VIII. It was accompanied by a punitive Act (1 Mary, Stat. 2, c. 3) against those who disturbed preachers or priests celebrating mass, or who sought to abuse the sacrament, deface altars and crucifixes, etc.

Forasmuch as by divers and several Acts hereafter mentioned, as well the divine service and good administration of the sacraments, as divers other matters of religion which we and our forefathers found in this Church of England, to us left by the authority of the Catholic Church, be partly altered and in some part taken from us, and in place thereof new things imagined and set forth by the said Acts, such as a few of singularity have of themselves devised, whereof hath ensued amongst us, in very short time, numbers of diverse and strange opinions and diversities of sects, and thereby grown great unquietness and much discord, to the great disturbance of the commonwealth of this realm, and in very short time like to grow to extreme peril and utter confusion of the same, unless some remedy be in that behalf provided, which thing all true, loving and obedient subjects ought and are bounden to foresee and provide, to the uttermost of their power.

[In consideration whereof, the following Acts are utterly repealed:

1 Edw. VI, c. 1,   concerning the Sacrament of the Altar. (**VII, 1**)

1 Edw. VI, c. 2,   concerning the Election of Bishops. (see **VII, 1**)

2 & 3 Edw. VI, c. 1,   the first Edwardian Act of Uniformity. (**VII, 5**)

2 & 3 Edw. VI, c. 21, to take away Laws against the Marriage of Priests. (**VII, 6**)

3 & 4 Edw. VI, c. 10, for abolishing divers Books and Images. (see **VII, 5**)

3 & 4 Edw. VI, c. 12, for the Ordering of Ecclesiastical Ministers.

5 & 6 Edw. VI, c. 1,   the second Edwardian Act of Uniformity. (**VII, 7**)

5 & 6 Edw. VI, c. 3,   for the Keeping of Holy-Days and Fasting Days. (see **IV, 1**)

5 & 6 Edw. VI, c. 12, a Declaratory Act for the Marriage of Priests and for the Legitimation of their Children.]

II   And be it further enacted by the authority aforesaid, that all such divine service and administration of sacraments as were most commonly used in the realm of England in the last year of the reign of our late Sovereign Lord King Henry VIII shall be, from and after the twentieth day of December in this present year of our Lord God 1553, used and frequented throughout the whole realm of England and all other the Queen's Majesty's dominions; and that no other kind nor order of divine service nor administration of sacraments be, after the said twentieth day of December, used or ministered in any other manner, form, or degree within the said realm of England, or other the Queen's dominions, than was most commonly used, ministered and frequented in the said last year of the reign of the said late King Henry VIII.

III   And be it further enacted by the authority aforesaid, that no person shall be impeached or molested in body or goods for using heretofore, or until the said twentieth day of December, the divine service mentioned in the said Acts or any of them, nor for the using of the old divine service and administration of sacraments, in such manner and form as was used in the Church of England before the making of any of the said Acts.

Stat. Realm, iv.202

2   The Marian Injunctions, 1554

The Queen sent these Injunctions to the bishops along with a letter (4 March 1554) ordering them to be enforced. The term sacramentary (item IV) was commonly used to denote a left-wing Protestant, especially one who held Zwinglian opinions on the eucharist, i.e. that Christ's words of institution at the Last Supper ('this is my body', etc.) had been intended only in a symbolic and figurative sense.

Perhaps the most important items are nos. VII-IX, directing the removal of married priests (see **VII, 6**) from their benefices. Ordinary secular priests, having done penance and undertaken to live apart from their wives, were qualified to receive a benefice in another place. 'Religious men', i.e. former members of religious orders who had taken an actual vow of chastity, were to be treated as more seriously guilty and a sentence of divorce pronounced against them. In certain dioceses (e.g. York), where the day-to-day records of the ecclesiastical courts have survived, it can be shown that these instructions were followed in detail over the next few months, and that a considerable number of clergy were deprived for marriage. In the diocese of York about a tenth of the beneficed parish clergy had married during the brief period between 1549 and 1553. In Essex, about 88 out of 319 beneficed priests were deprived, and though this area was more exposed to Protestant influences, by no means all of these clerics appear to have been ardent Protestants.

Item XV impugns the validity of holy orders received under the Edwardian Prayer Books (see **VII, 7**) and vaguely allows the bishops to 'supply that thing which wanted in them before'; yet the known deprivations were carried out in almost every case on account of marriage and not on the charge of defective ordination.

I   That every bishop and his officers, with all other having ecclesiastical jurisdiction, shall with all speed and diligence, and all manner of ways to them possible, put in execution all such canons and ecclesiastical laws heretofore in the time of King Henry VIII used within this realm of England, and the dominions of the same, not being direct and expressly contrary to the laws and statutes of this realm.

II   Item, that no bishop, or any his officer, or other person aforesaid, hereafter in any of their ecclesiastical writings in process, or other extra-judicial acts, do use to put in this clause or sentence: *Regia auctoritate fulcitus* [sanctioned by royal authority].

III   Item, that no bishop, or any his officers, or other person aforesaid, do hereafter exact or demand in the admission of any person to any ecclesiastical promotion, order, or office, any oath touching the primacy or succession, as of late, in few years past, has been accustomed and used.

IV Item, that every bishop and his officers, with all other persons aforesaid, have a vigilant eye, and use special diligence and foresight, that no person be admitted or received to any ecclesiastical function, benefice, or office, being a sacramentary, infected or defamed with any notable kind of heresy or other great crime; and that the said bishop do stay, and cause to be stayed, as much as lieth in him, that benefices and ecclesiastical promotions do not notably decay, or take hindrance, by passing or confirming of unreasonable leases.

V Item, that every bishop, and all other persons aforesaid, do diligently travail for the repressing of heresies and notable crimes, especially in the clergy, duly correcting and punishing the same.

VI Item, that every bishop, and all other persons aforesaid, do likewise travail for the condemning and repressing of corrupt and naughty [wicked] opinions, unlawful books, ballads, and other pernicious and hurtful devices, engendering hatred among the people, and discord among the same; and that schoolmasters, preachers, and teachers do exercise and use their offices and duties without teaching, preaching, or setting forth any evil or corrupt doctrine; and that, doing the contrary, they may be, by the bishop and his said officers, punished and removed.

VII Item, that every bishop, and all the other persons aforesaid, proceeding summarily, and with all celerity and speed, may and shall deprive, or declare deprived, and amove, according to their learning and discretion, all such persons from their benefices and ecclesiastical promotions, who, contrary to the state of their order and the laudable custom of the Church, have married and used women as their wives, or otherwise notably and slanderously disordered or abused themselves; sequestering also, during the said process, the fruits and profits of the said benefices and ecclesiastical promotions.

VIII Item, that the said bishop, and all other persons aforesaid, do use more lenity and clemency with such as have married, whose wives be dead, than with others whose women do yet remain in life; and likewise such priests as, with the consents of their wives or women, openly in the presence of the bishop, do profess to abstain, to be used the more favourably: in which case, after penance effectually done, the bishop, according to his discretion and wisdom, may, upon just consideration, receive and admit them again to their former administration, so it be not in the same place; appointing them such a portion to live upon, to be paid out of their benefice, whereof they be deprived, by discretion of the said bishop, or his officers, as they shall think may be spared of the said benefice.

IX   Item, that every bishop, and all persons aforesaid, do foresee that they suffer not any religious man, having solemnly professed chastity, to continue with his woman or wife; but that all such persons, after deprivation of their benefice or ecclesiastical promotion, be also divorced every one from his said woman, and due punishment otherwise taken for the offence therein.

X   Item, that every bishop, and all other persons aforesaid, do take order and direction with the parishioners of every benefice where priests do want [are lacking], to repair to the next parish for divine service; or to appoint for a convenient time, till other better provision may be made, one curate to serve [alternately] in divers parishes, and to allot to the said curate for his labour some portion of the benefice that he so serves.

XI   Item, that all and all manner of processions of the Church be used, frequented, and continued after the old order of the Church, in the Latin tongue.

XII   Item, that all such holy-days and fasting days be observed and kept, as was observed and kept in the latter time of King Henry VIII.

XIII   Item, that the laudable and honest ceremonies which were wont to be used, frequented, and observed in the Church, be also hereafter frequented, used and observed.

XIV   Item, that children be christened by the priest, and confirmed by the bishops, as heretofore hath been accustomed and used.

XV   Item, touching such persons as were heretofore promoted to any orders after the new sort and fashion of order, considering they were not ordered in very deed, the bishop of the diocese finding otherwise sufficiency and ability in those men, may supply that thing which wanted in them before; and then, according to his discretion, admit them to minister.

XVI   Item, that, by the bishop of the diocese, a uniform doctrine be set forth by homilies, or otherwise, for the good instruction and teaching of all people; and that the said bishop, and other persons aforesaid, do compel the parishioners to come to their several churches, and there devoutly to hear divine service, as of reason they ought.

XVII Item, that they examine all schoolmasters and teachers of children, and finding them suspect in any wise, to remove them, and place Catholic men in their rooms, with a special commandment to instruct their children, so as they may be able to answer the priest at the Mass, and so help the priest to Mass as has been accustomed.

XVIII Item, that the said bishop, and all other the persons aforesaid, have such regard, respect and consideration of and for the setting forth of the premises with all kind of virtue, godly living, and good example, with repressing also and keeping under of vice and unthriftiness, as they and every of them may be seen to favour the restitution of true religion; and also to make an honest account and reckoning of their office and cure to the honour of God, our good contentation, and the profit of this realm and dominions of the same.

> Gee and Hardy, pp. 380-3, from Bonner's
> Register, fo. 342b

3   The Heresy Acts Revived, 1554
(1 & 2 Philip & Mary, c. 6)

By the following Act Mary's third Parliament (November 1554-January 1555) revived the medieval legislation against heresy: 5 Ric. II, Stat. 2, c. 5; 2 Hen. IV, c. 15; 2 Hen. V, St. 1, c. 7. The repeals of these under Henry VIII and Edward VI are not mentioned. Serious persecution began immediately. The first martyr, John Rogers (*alias* Thomas Matthew, see **VI, 2**), was burned on 4 February 1555, Dr. Rowland Taylor and Bishop Hooper on 9 February.

For the eschewing and avoiding of errors and heresies, which of late have risen, grown and much increased within this realm, for that the ordinaries* have wanted [lacked] authority to proceed against those that were infected therewith: be it therefore ordained and enacted by authority of this present Parliament, that the Statute made in the fifth year of the reign of King Richard II, concerning the arresting and apprehension of erroneous and heretical preachers, and one other Statute made in the second year of the reign of King Henry IV, concerning the repressing of heresies and punishment of heretics, and also one other Statute made in the second year of the reign of King Henry V, concerning the suppression of heresy and Lollardy, and every article, branch, and sentence contained in the same three several Acts, and

every of them, shall from the twentieth day of January next coming
be revived, and be in full force, strength, and effect to all intents, constructions and purposes for ever.

Stat. Realm, iv.244

4 Mary's Second Statute of Repeal, 1554 (1 & 2 Philip & Mary, c. 8)

Like the preceding item, this Act was agreed by Mary's third Parliament before
the end of 1554. On 29 November Parliament approved a petition for reconciliation with Rome and the following day the King and Queen received
absolution from the Legate, Cardinal Pole. This subsequent second Statute of
Repeal, which came into force on 20 January 1555, abolished all Acts passed
against the Papacy since the beginning of the Reformation Parliament in 1529.
But so far from repealing the Dissolution Acts, it devotes many clauses to safe-
guarding the rights of the holders of former monastic lands. It has thus the
character of a bargain between Queen Mary and the governing classes.
Pole is here described as Legate *de latere* (usually *a latere*), i.e. one sent direct
'from the side' of the Pope and charged with a special mission.

Whereas since the 20th year of King Henry the Eighth of famous
memory, father unto your Majesty our most natural Sovereign and
gracious Lady and Queen, much false and erroneous doctrine hath
been taught, preached, and written, partly by divers the natural-born
subjects of this realm, and partly being brought in hither from sundry
other foreign countries, hath been sown and spread abroad within the
same; by reason whereof as well the spiritualty as the temporalty of
your Highness's realms and dominions have swerved from the obedience of the See Apostolic and declined from the unity of Christ's
Church, and so have continued, until such time as your Majesty being
first raised up by God and set in the seat royal over us, and then by his
divine and gracious Providence knit in marriage with the most noble
and virtuous prince, the King our Sovereign Lord your husband, the
Pope's Holiness and the See Apostolic sent hither unto your Majesties
(as unto persons undefiled and by God's goodness preserved from the
common infection aforesaid) and to the whole realm, the most
Reverend Father in God the Lord Cardinal Pole, Legate *de latere*, to
call us home again into the right way, from whence we have all this
long while wandered and strayed abroad: and we after sundry long

and grievous plagues and calamities, seeing by the goodness of God our own errors, have acknowledged the same unto the said most Reverend Father, and by him have been and are the rather at the contemplation of your Majesties received and embraced into the unity and bosom of Christ's Church; and upon our humble submission and promise made, for a declaration of our repentance, to repeal and abrogate such acts and statutes as had been made in Parliament since the said 20th year of the said King Henry the Eighth, against the Supremacy of the See Apostolic, as in our submission exhibited to the said most Reverend Father in God by your Majesties appeareth: the tenor whereof ensueth:

We the Lords spiritual and temporal and the Commons assembled in this present Parliament, representing the whole body of the realm of England and the dominions of the same, in the name of ourselves particularly and also of the said body universally in this our supplication directed to your Majesties, with most humble suit that it may by your Graces' intercession and mean [mediation] be exhibited to the most Reverend Father in God the Lord Cardinal Pole, Legate sent specially hither from our most Holy Father the Pope Julius the Third and the See Apostolic of Rome, do declare ourselves very sorry and repentant of the schism and disobedience committed in this realm and dominions aforesaid against the said See Apostolic, either by making, agreeing, or executing any laws, ordinances, or commandments against the Supremacy of the said See, or otherwise doing or speaking that might impugn the same; offering ourselves and promising by this our supplication that for a token and knowledge of our said repentance we be and shall be always ready, under and with the authorities of your Majesties, to the utmost of our powers, to do that shall lie in us for the abrogation and repealing of the said laws and ordinances in this present Parliament as well for ourselves as for the whole body whom we represent. Whereupon we most humbly desire your Majesties, as personages undefiled in the offence of this body towards the said See, which nevertheless God by his Providence hath made subject to you, to set forth this our most humble suit that we may obtain from the See Apostolic by the said most Reverend Father, as well particularly as generally, absolution, release, and discharge from all danger of such censures and sentences as by the laws of the Church we be fallen into; and that we may as children repentant be received into the bosom and unity of Christ's Church, so as this noble realm with all the members thereof may in this unity and perfect obedience to the See Apostolic and Popes for the time being serve God and your Majesties to the furtherance and advancement of his honour and glory. We are at the intercession of your Majesties by the authority of our Holy Father Pope Julius the Third and of the See Apostolic assoiled [absolved], discharged, and delivered from excommunication, interdictions, and other censures ecclesiastical which hath hanged over our heads for our said defaults since the time of the said schism mentioned in our supplication. It may now like your Majesties that for the accomplishment of our promise made in the said supplication, that is to repeal all laws and statutes made contrary to the said Supremacy and See Apostolic during the said schism, the which is to be understood since the 20th year of the reign of the said late King Henry the Eighth, and so the said Lord Legate doth accept and recognise the same.

[II-VII The following Acts or parts of Acts are now repealed:

The part of 21 Hen. VIII, c. 13, which forbade the procuring from Rome of Dispensations* for pluralities* or non-residence*.

23 Hen. VIII, c. 9,   in Restraint of Citations.

24 Hen. VIII, c. 12, in Restraint of Appeals. (**III, 5**).

23 Hen. VIII, c. 20, in Conditional Restraint of Annates* and concerning the Consecration of Bishops. (**III, 4**)

25 Hen. VIII, c. 19, for the Submission of the Clergy. (see **III, 3**)

25 Hen. VIII, c. 20, in Absolute Restraint of Annates and concerning the Election of Bishops. (**III, 6**)

25 Hen. VIII, c. 21, forbidding Papal Dispensations and Payment of Peter's Pence. (**III, 7**)

26 Hen. VIII, c. 1,   The Act of Supremacy. (**III, 8**)

26 Hen. VIII, c. 14, for the Consecration of Suffragans.

27 Hen. VIII, c. 15, for the Appointment of a Commission for the making of Ecclesiastical Laws.

28 Hen. VIII, c. 10, extinguishing the Authority of the Bishop of Rome. (see **III, 7**)

28 Hen. VIII, c. 16, to release those obtaining pretended Licences and Dispensations from the see of Rome.

The part of 28 Hen. VIII, c. 7,   (one of the Acts of Succession) which
provided that persons marrying within
the prohibited degrees should be separ-
ated by the episcopal courts, without
appeal to Rome.

31 Hen. VIII, c. 9,   Authorising the King to erect new
Bishoprics.

32 Hen. VIII, c. 38,   Concerning pre-contracts of marriage
and degrees of consanguinity.

35 Hen. VIII, c. 3,   Concerning the King's Style.

The part of 35 Hen. VIII, c. 1,   (one of the Acts of Succession) which
had imposed an Oath of Supremacy.

37 Hen. VIII, c. 17,   entitled 'An act that the Doctors of the
Civil Law may exercise ecclesiastical
jurisdiction'.

Those parts of 5 and 6 Edw. VI, c. 12,   which had assigned penalties
for preaching against the Royal
Supremacy or Affirming that the
Bishop of Rome is Supreme Head.]

VIII   And be it further enacted by the authority aforesaid that all
clauses, sentences, and articles of every other statute or act of Parliament
made since the said 20th year of the reign of King Henry the Eighth
against the Supreme authority of the Pope's Holiness or See Apostolic
of Rome, or containing any other matter of the same effect only, that
is repealed in any of the statutes aforesaid, shall be also by authority
hereof from henceforth utterly void, frustrate, and of none effect.

IX   ... And, finally, where certain acts and statutes have been made
in the time of the late schism concerning the lands and hereditaments
of archbishoprics and bishoprics, the suppression and dissolution of
monasteries, abbeys, priories, chantries*, colleges, and all other the
pgods and chattels of religious houses, since the which time the right
bad dominion of certain lands and hereditaments, goods and chattels,
oelonging to the same be dispersed abroad and come to the hands and
nossessions of divers and sundry persons who by gift, purchase, ex-
change, and other means, according to the order of the laws and
statutes of this realm for the time being, have the same: for the avoiding of all scruples that might grow by any the occasions aforesaid or by
any other ways or means whatsoever, it may please your Majesties to
be intercessors and mediators to the said most Reverend Father Car-

dinal Pole, that all such causes and quarrels as by pretence of the said schism or by any other occasion or mean whatsoever might be moved, by the Pope's Holiness or See Apostolic or by any other jurisdiction ecclesiastical, may be utterly removed and taken away; so as all persons having sufficient conveyance of the said lands and hereditaments, goods and chattels, as is aforesaid by the common laws, acts, or statutes of this realm, may without scruple of conscience enjoy them, without impeachment or trouble by pretence of any General Council, canons, or ecclesiastical laws, and clear from all dangers of the censures of the Church.

[X and XI   There follow the texts of (1) a Supplication of the clergy to Cardinal Pole, urging him to leave in possession of the new owners the goods and rights of the Church alienated in the recent schism, but pleading for the full restoration of ecclesiastical jurisdiction to the clergy, and (2) a Dispensation from Pole, dated 24 December 1554, which ratifies the foundations (during the schism) of cathedrals, hospitals and schools; consents to 'receive in their orders and benefices' persons ordained and instituted 'by pretended authority of the Supremacy of the English Church'; agrees to ratify the sentences of ecclesiastical courts and confirm the titles of ecclesiastical property alienated. In respect of the divisions of bishoprics and the erection of cathedrals, the Pope's confirmation must, however, be asked. Pole's Dispensation ends by beseeching the new owners of ecclesiastical property to make due provision for the maintenance of parish clergy.

XII–XXIV   The text of the Act continues with a prayer of the Lords and Commons that this Dispensation may be confirmed in Parliament. They recall the acquisition of ecclesiastical property by Henry VIII, Edward VI, and other persons and corporate bodies, whose titles are to be freely confirmed in Parliament: persons attempting to disquiet them will incur the penalties of *Praemunire**. The title of Supreme Head, however unlawfully assumed, shall not impugn the validity of grants made by the Crown. The Act making void papal bulls is repealed. Whereas certain former monastic churches and chapels have been exempt from episcopal jurisdiction, the new lay owners shall not exercise local jurisdiction over them, and it shall revert to the bishops. This Act shall not diminish the privileges of the two Universities. To increase public devotion, owners may during the next 20 years grant lands, titles, etc., to religious foundations without obtaining royal licence. Papal and episcopal jurisdiction shall be as in the 20th year of Henry VIII, i.e. 22 April 1528-21 April 1529]

★   ★   ★

Stat. Realm, iv.246-54

5   Knox and Cox at Frankfurt

A Brief Discourse of the Troubles begun at Frankfurt, first published by a group of English Puritans in 1574, used to be ascribed to William Whittingham (Dean of Durham 1563-79), but is now thought to have been written by his close companion Thomas Wood. Soon after their arrival at Frankfurt-am-Main (June 1554), Whittingham and his friends were allowed the use of a church and allowed to regulate their own religious affairs. They remodelled the Second Edwardian Prayer Book (1552) along Calvinist lines, summoned John Knox from Geneva and made him their leader. Thomas Lever and other English exiles in Frankfurt, who favoured the retention of the Anglican forms of service, made no headway against the Knoxians until the arrival in March 1555 of the formidable Dr. Richard Cox. The latter was already famous as the Vice-chancellor who had established Protestantism in Oxford under Edward VI. From this point there occurred a confrontation – prophetic of so much later religious history in England – between the Calvinist Knoxians, and the Coxians who 'would have the face of an English Church'. Inside a fortnight the Coxians, using the discreditable stratagem described below, induced the Frankfurt authorities to expel Knox, who retired to the more congenial exile of Geneva.

At which time (13 March 1555) Doctor Cox and others with him came to Frankfurt out of England; who began to break that Order which was agreed upon: first in answering aloud after the minister [making the responses], contrary to the church's determination; and being admonished thereof by the seniors of the congregation, he with the rest that came with him made answer that they would do as they had done in England; and that they would have the face of an English Church.

And the Sunday following one of his company, without the consent and knowledge of the congregation, got up suddenly into the pulpit, read the Litany, and Doctor Cox and his company answered aloud, whereby the determination of the church was broken.

The same Sunday, at afternoon, it came to Master Knox his turn to preach, who having passed so far in *Genesis* that he was come to Noah as he lay open in his tent, he spake these words following: 'As divers things . . . ought to be kept secret, even so such things as tend to the dishonour of God and disquieting of his Church ought to be disclosed and openly reproved!'

And thereon he showed how after long trouble and contention among them a godly agreement was made, and how that the same, that day, was ungodly broken, which thing became not, as he said, the proudest of them all to have attempted. Alleging furthermore that like as by the word of God we must seek our warrant for the establishing of religion, and without that to thrust nothing into any Christian congregation, so (forasmuch as in the English Book were things both superstitious, unpure and unperfect, which he offered to prove before all men) he would not consent that of that church it should be received: and that in case men would go about to burden that free congregation therewith, so oft as he [Knox] should come in that place, the text offering occasion, he would not fail to speak against it.

He farther affirmed that, among many things which provoked God's anger against England, slackness to reform religion, when time and place was granted, was one: and therefore it became them to be circumspect how they laid their foundation. And where some men ashamed not to say, that there was no let [hindrance] or stop in England, but that religion might be, and was already, brought to perfection, he proved the contrary:

By the want of discipline:
Also by the troubles which Master Hooper sustained for the rochet [surplice worn by a bishop] and such like in the [Prayer] Book commanded and allowed:
And for that one man was permitted to have three, four or five benefices, to the great slander of the gospel, and defrauding of the flock of Christ of their lively food and sustenance.

These were the chief notes of his sermon, which was so stomached [resented] of some (especially of such as had many livings in England) that he was very sharply charged and reproved, so soon as he came out of the pulpit for the same.

[The Knox party continued to press for the abolition of the Litany, the responses, the *Te Deum* and other parts of the Prayer Book. Cox refused these concessions and Whittingham induced the Frankfurt magistrates to threaten Cox's party with expulsion if they failed to conform. Just when all seemed desperate for the Coxians one of them, Edward Isaac, devised the following stratagem.]

Nevertheless such as would so fain have had the Book of England, left not the matter thus. And for that they saw Knox to be in such credit with many of the congregation, they first of all assayed by a most cruel, barbarous and bloody practice to dispatch him out of the way, to the end they might with more ease attain the thing which they so greedily sought, which was the placing of their Book [the establishing of the Second Edwardian Prayer Book].

They had among them a book of his, entitled *An Admonition to Christians*, written in the English tongue, wherein by occasion he spake of the Emperor, Philip his son, and of Mary, then Queen of England. This book certain of them presented to the magistrates [of Frankfurt] who, upon receipt of the same sent for Whittingham, and asked him of Knox their minister what manner of man he was. Whittingham answered that such a one there was among them, and to his knowledge both a learned, wise, grave and godly man. Then one of the magistrates said unto him, 'Certain of your countrymen have accused him unto us *Laesae Majestatis Imperatoriae*, that is of high treason against the Emperor, his son and the Queen of England. Here is the book and the places which they have noted. The true and perfect sense we command you . . . to bring unto us in the Latin tongue, at one of the clock in the afternoon.' Which thing he did accordingly. At which time, after certain communication among themselves, they commanded that Knox should preach no more till their pleasure were further known. . . .

[Knox's own account shows us that eight insulting passages of his *Admonition* were being cited, of which the most important was one claiming that the Emperor 'is no less enemy to Christ than was Nero'.]

But it seemed the magistrates abhorred this bloody, cruel and outrageous attempt. For that when as certain of Knox's enemies followed hardly [closely] the magistrates, to know what should be done with him, they did not only show the most evident signs of disliking their unnatural suit, but also sent for Masters Williams and Whittingham, willing them that Master Knox should depart the city. For otherwise, as they said, they should be forced to deliver him, if the Emperor's Council, which then lay at Augsburg, should, upon like information, send for him. The 25th of March [1555] Master Knox, being the night before his departure, made a most comfortable sermon at his lodging to fifty persons or thereabout then present; which sermon was of the death and resurrection of Christ, and of the unspeakable joys which were prepared for God's Elect, which in this life suffer trouble and persecution for testimony of his blessed name. The next day he was brought three or four miles in his way by some of those unto whom, the night before, he had made that exhortation, who with great heaviness of heart and plenty of tears committed him to the Lord.

A Brief Discourse of the Troubles at Frankfurt, ed. E. Arber (1908), pp. 54-61

6   (a) (b) and (c) The Protestant Congregation in London

These three extracts afford a picture of the secret London congregation during the Marian persecution. Thomas Bentham (Bishop of Coventry and Lichfield, 1560-79) confirms the story of the Protestant demonstration at Smithfield in a letter to Thomas Lever. The martyrs, he writes, 'were so mightily spoken unto, so comfortably taken by the hand, and so godly comforted, notwithstanding that fearful proclamation and the present threatenings of the sheriff and sergeants that the adversaries themselves were astonished'.

Of the other ministers mentioned, the Scotsman John Rough had been a prominent associate of Knox and was martyred at Smithfield in December 1557. 'Thomas Simson' may be an error for the deacon and martyr Cuthbert Simpson. Along with John Rough there was burned one of his flock, Margaret Mearing: the author of our extract (b) appears to have been her husband, probably anxious to exculpate himself by giving information. On the other hand Roger Sergeant, the author of (c), seems to have attached himself to the Protestant congregation and systematically disclosed their affairs to Bishop Bonner. His description confirms the essentially Anglican character of the group, and its use of the Prayer Book of 1552.

(a) A GENERAL ACCOUNT BY JOHN FOXE

No less marvellous was the preservation of the congregation in London, which from the first beginning of Queen Mary to the latter end thereof continued, notwithstanding whatsoever the malice, device, searching and inquisition of men, or strictness of laws could work to the contrary.... Of this great bountiful goodness of the Lord, many and great examples appeared in the congregation which now I speak of. How oft and in what great danger did he deliver them!

First at the Blackfriars, where they should have resorted to Sir Thomas Carden's house, privy watch was laid for them; but yet, through the Lord's vigilant providence, the mischief was prevented, and they [were] delivered. Again, how narrowly did they escape about Aldgate, where spies were laid for them; and had not Thomas Simson the deacon espied them, and bid them disperse themselves away, they had been taken. For within two hours the constable coming to the house after they were gone, demanded of the wife what company had been there. To whom she, to excuse the matter, made answer again, saying that half-a-dozen good fellows had been there at breakfast, as they went a-maying. Another time also, about the great Conduit they, passing there through a very strait alley into a clothworker's loft, were espied and the sheriffs sent for: but before they came, they, having privy knowledge thereof, immediately shifted away out of the alley....

Betwixt Radcliffe and Rotherhithe, in a ship called Jesus Ship, twice or thrice they assembled, having there closely after their accustomed manner both sermon, prayer and communion; and yet, through the protection of the Lord, they returned, though not unespied, yet untaken.... But they never escaped more hardly, than once in Thames Street in the night-time, where the house being beset with enemies, yet, as the Lord would, they were delivered by the means of a mariner, who being at that present in the same company, and seeing no other way to avoid, plucked off his slops [loose trousers] and swam to the next boat, and so rowed the company over, using his shoes instead of oars....

In this church or congregation there were sometimes forty, sometimes a hundred, sometimes two hundred, sometimes more and sometimes less. About the latter time of Queen Mary it greatly increased. From the first beginning ... they had divers ministers: first Master Scamler, then Thomas Fowle, after him Master Rough, then Master Augustine Bernher, then last Master Bentham, concerning the deliverance of which Master Bentham (being now Bishop of Coventry and Lichfield), God's mighty providence most notably is to be considered....

At what time [28 July 1558] the seven last burnt at Smithfield ... were condemned and brought to the stake to suffer, came down in the name of the King and Queen a proclamation, being twice pronounced openly to the people (first at Newgate, then at the stake where they should suffer) straitly charging and commanding that no man should either pray for them, or speak to them, or once say, God help them. It was appointed before, of the godly there standing together, which was a great multitude, that so soon as the prisoners should be brought, they should go to them to embrace and to comfort them; and so they did. For as the said martyrs were coming towards the place in the people's sight, being brought with bills and glaves [bladed weapons] as the custom is, the godly multitude and congregation with a general sway made towards the prisoners, in such manner that the billmen and the other officers, being all thrust back, could nothing do, nor any thing come nigh. So the godly people meeting and embracing, and kissing them, brought them in their arms (which might as easily have conveyed them clean away) unto the place where they should suffer.

This done, and the people giving place to the officers, the proclamation with a loud voice was read to the people . . . that no man should pray for them, or once speak a word unto them, etc. Master Bentham, the minister then of the congregation, not sparing for that, but as zeal and Christian charity moved him, and seeing the fire set to them, turning his eyes to the people, cried and said, 'We know they are the people of God, and therefore we cannot choose but wish well to them, and say, God strengthen them!' With that all the people with a whole consent and one voice followed and said, 'Amen, Amen!' The noise whereof was so great, and the cries thereof so many, that the officers could not tell what to say, or whom to accuse.

Foxe, viii.558–9

(b) THE INFORMATION OF JAMES MEARING

Cuthbert [Simpson] is an officer or deacon in the assembly, a rich man dwelling in London. Cluney [one of Bishop Bonner's officers] doth know him. He is paymaster to the prisoners in the Marshalsea, Ludgate, Lollards' Tower [at St Paul's] and in other places of prison as the Compter, etc., and executor to the prisoners that die, and collector of the assembly when the reading is done, and had the goods of James and his wife, that were burned at Islington. And likewise one Brook in Queenhithe, salter and seller of earthern pots; a rich man, not coming to church; a collector also, and keeper of the money for the prisoners. Mistress Barber in Fish Street, a fishmonger's wife; Cluney knoweth her; she is also a collector for the said prisoners.

The meeting sometimes is at Wapping, at one Church's house, hard by the water side; sometimes at a widow's house at Ratcliffe, at the King's Head there; sometimes at St. Katherine's, at a shoemaker's house, a Dutchman called Frogg. . . . Sometimes the assembly beginneth at seven in the morning, or at eight; sometimes at nine; and then or soon after they dine and tarry till two of the clock, and amongst other things they talk and make officers. Sometimes the assembly is at Battle Bridge, at a dyer's house betwixt two butchers there; despising the sacrament of the altar, the Pope, the coming to church and the priest. In that assembly there are a minister and two priests that gather money.

Foxe, viii.459

(c) THE INFORMATION OF ROGER SERGEANT GIVEN TO THE BISHOP OF LONDON AND HIS OFFICERS . . . WHEREBY MANY WERE APPREHENDED

Roger Sergeant, born in Buckinghamshire, tailor of the age of forty years or above, now of the parish of St. Edmund's in Lombard Street, saith that at the Swan at Limehouse, or else at St. Katherine's at one Frogg's, or at the King's Head at Ratcliffe, the assembly shall be on the third Sunday of Advent between nine and eleven aforenoon and from one till four at afternoon. And sometimes the meeting is at Horsleydown beyond Battle Bridge. Commonly the usage is to have all the English service without any diminishing, wholly as it was in the time of King Edward VI, neither praying for the King nor the Queen, despising the sacrament of the altar, and the coming to church, saying that a man cannot come to the church, except he be a partaker of all the evils there. They have reading and preaching, and the minister is a Scotchman, whose name he knoweth not [John Rough]; and they have two deacons that gather money, which is distributed to the prisoners in the Marshalsea, King's Bench, Lollards' Tower, Newgate, and to the poor that come to the assembly; some women be childbearing and some women above sixty years of age, and divers coming more for money than for aught else. This informer hath been there twice and no more; but he will go thither again, that such as shall be sent to apprehend the malefactors may know the places and persons. [The informer then lists various members of the congregation, including a smith, a cobbler, a butcher, a tailor and a silk-dyer.]

Foxe, viii.458

7   Protestants in Colchester

The following report by the priest Thomas Tye is addressed to Bonner, in whose diocese Essex lay. Another informer, Stephen Morris, mentions three Protestant clerics who moved to and fro between the London and Colchester congregations. One of them was John Pulleyne, formerly rector of St. Peter's, Cornhill, who escaped to Geneva in 1557; another, Simon Harlestone, was brother-in-law of the future Archbishop Matthew Parker. Of the Colchester people here mentioned, William and Alice Mount and Rose Allin were all burned there, along with seven others, in April 1557.

Right honourable lord, . . . these shall be to signify unto your lordship the state of our parts concerning religion. And first, since the coming down of the twenty-two rank heretics dismissed from you, the detestable sort of schismatics were never so bold since the King and Queen's Majesties' reign, as they are now at this present. In Much Bentley, where your lordship is patron of the church, since William Mount and Alice his wife, with Rose Allin her daughter came home, they do not only absent themselves from the church and service of God, but do daily allure many other away from the same, which before did outwardly show signs and tokens of obedience.

They assemble together upon the Sabbath day in the time of divine service, sometimes in one house, sometimes in another, and there keep their privy conventicles and schools of heresy. . . . Your officers say . . . that the Council sent them not home without a great consideration. I pray God some of your officers prove not favourers of heretics. The rebels are stout in the town of Colchester. The ministers of the church are hemmed at in the open streets and called knaves. The blessed sacrament of the altar is blasphemed and railed upon in every house and tavern. Prayer and fasting are not regarded. Seditious talks and news are rife, both in town and country, in as ample and large manner as though there had no honourable lords and commissioners been sent for reformation thereof. The occasion riseth partly by reason of John Love of Colchester Heath, a perverse place; which John Love was twice indicted of heresy and thereupon fled with his wife and household, and his goods seized within the town of Colchester. . . . Nevertheless the said John is come home again, and nothing said or done to him. Whereupon the heretics are wonderfully encouraged, to the no little discomfort of good and Catholic people, which daily pray to God for the profit, unity and restoration of his Church again; which thing shall come the sooner to pass, through the travail and pains of such honourable lords and reverend fathers as your lordship is, unto whom I wish long life and continuance, with increase of much honour. From Colchester the 18th of December [1556].

Your humble beadsman

Thomas Tye, priest

Foxe, viii.383

EPILOGUE

The Elizabethan Settlement of 1559 restored the Royal Supremacy over the English Church, though Elizabeth assumed the title of 'Supreme Governor'. It also re-established the Second English Prayer Book of 1552 with a few significant amendments: in effect these allowed a considerable degree of latitude in eucharistic belief. All except one of the depleted bench of Marian bishops rejected the Settlement, but the vast majority of the 9000 or so parochial clergy conformed with very little overt protest. (See **VII, 8.**) In 1563 the Settlement was completed by a revised formulary of faith, the Thirty-nine Articles (see **Introduction**, pp. 11-12), which received statutory confirmation in 1571. This Settlement, apart from its displacement for a short time in the mid-seventeenth century, has survived in substantially the same form through four centuries. At the time of its origins, however, it represented a rather uneasy compromise between the somewhat radical Protestantism of the 1559 House of Commons, mainly inspired by the returning Coxian exiles (see **VIII, 5**), and the extremely conservative Protestantism of the Queen, largely guided by secular motives of a *politique* nature. As we can now see, these two approaches were hard to reconcile, and the likelihood of heavy criticism from within the Church itself was thus inherent in the situation from the very outset. This naturally increased under the influence of the Knoxian exiles (see **VIII, 5**), who returned to England after the Settlement had been agreed. Throughout Elizabeth's reign continuous demands were in fact made by a conscientious and highly articulate minority for sweeping changes in the 'externals' of worship (e.g. the type of vestments to be worn), and in the government, ritual and liturgy of the Church. The aim was to 'purify' (hence the word 'puritan') the nationally-established Church, to purge it of what were considered to be medieval accretions and Romish practices. Simultaneously, the Catholic challenge to the Settlement grew, especially after the Jesuits and seminary priests began their missionary work in England.

Nevertheless, by the end of Elizabeth's reign, both these threats to the Settlement had been effectively contained, partly by repressive measures, partly because the Puritan movement was itself divided between moderates and militants, and partly because the fight for national survival against Spain had occupied the attention and secured the loyalty of the great majority of Puritan and Catholic subjects alike. Indeed, during the reign Protestantism became increasingly identified with the national cause, a development assisted by the publication of John Foxe's immensely popular *Acts and Monuments* (commonly known as Foxe's *Book of Martyrs*), from which a number of our extracts have been drawn. A corollary to this development was a popular hatred of Rome which lasted for generations. At the same time Puritanism, considered as a mental discipline and apart from its ecclesiastical aspects, invaded the English temperament and henceforth exercised a marked influence upon the nation.

The events of the seventeenth century were to make it manifestly clear that the ideal of a fully comprehensive Settlement had failed: the final outcome was that the English produced not merely a State-Church but a whole series of churches and sects, many of which flourished in New England and other parts of the American continent. Here in England, by the end of the seventeenth century Protestant Dissenters of all denominations except the Unitarians were enjoying liberty of worship, though in political life they long continued to be second-class citizens, being as yet barred from civil office and from the two universities. It should be said that this toleration arose for the most part out of political expediency, though there were minorities – discernible even in the sixteenth century – which with varying emphasis advocated religious toleration as a principle drawn from gospel Christianity.

It was not until the last quarter of the eighteenth century that statutory measures began to be taken which relieved Catholics from the risks of persecution, but since 1714 there had in fact been little active persecution in England. From about this time the religious temperature dropped considerably and society became increasingly concerned with its secular interests. Yet it was during this same period, often called the 'Age of Reason', that the Anglican Church was again submitted to scrutiny from within, in the forms of both Methodism and the Evangelical Movement. One of the main aims of both was to ensure that the Church should conduct a more effective ministry: the failure here was particularly evident in regard to the poorer elements of the growing industrial populations of the towns. In the event, John Wesley's intense demand for a more explicit and fervent evangel led to further divisions in English religion, which are only in process of being healed in our own day.

Such observations might seem to suggest that the fissiparous tendency of Protestantism, with its important repercussions throughout the world, was the most significant outcome of the English Reformation. This does not follow. The Anglican Church itself, based largely on the Elizabethan Settlement, simultaneously underwent a process of consolidation, despite its merely gradual success in imposing many of the reforms demanded at the time of the Reformation. Several factors underlay this process: the publication (1594-7) of Richard Hooker's *Ecclesiastical Polity*, a theological and philosophical defence of the Elizabethan Settlement; the increasing affection accorded to Cranmer's Prayer Book; the tendency of many English men and women to be drawn toward a Church which gradually broadened its doctrinal sympathies and which could tolerate within itself a wide diversity of emphases. The germ of this religious liberalism can be seen in the adiaphorist* approach which we observed at work in some English minds as far back as the 1530s.

GLOSSARY

ADIAPHORIST (ISM): (from Greek *adiaphora*, 'things indifferent'). The principle that in certain matters of doctrine and ritual a variety of belief and interpretation may be tolerated, without prejudice to fundamentals.

ANABAPTISTS: The name given to a variety of groups, mostly on the Continent but present in small numbers in England from about 1534. They upheld free will, and rejected infant baptism, replacing it by baptism of believers. Everywhere they were severely persecuted by both Protestants and Catholics, largely because they denied the right of the civil authority to decide religious matters, to compel them to take oaths, bear arms, etc.

ANNATES (OR FIRST FRUITS): See pp. 51-2 and 65-6.

APPROPRIATION(S), APPROPRIATE(D): See p. 3, and also IMPROPRIATIONS and TITHES below.

CHANTRY: See p. 127, and also PURGATORY below. In connection with some chantries, a special chapel had been erected in the parish church.

DISPENSATION(S): See p. 60.

ERASTIAN (ISM): The theory that the Church should be directed by, and subordinated to, the secular power. The word derives from the name of the Swiss theologian Thomas Erastus (1524-83), but the viewpoint had been expressed by a number of authors (notably Marsiglio of Padua, d. 1342) from the fourteenth century. See also p. 7 and p. 46.

FIRST FRUITS: See ANNATES.

IMPROPRIATION(S): After the Dissolution many benefices previously held by monasteries (Appropriations) were assigned to lay proprietors: this is usually referred to as Impropriation. (But in I, 4, Sir Francis Bigod uses the word 'impropriation' even though he is speaking about monasteries.) See also TITHES below.

JUSTIFICATION BY FAITH ALONE (or SOLIFIDIANISM): The doctrine that man is put in a saving relationship with God solely by faith, and not by good works or by any merits of his own. See also pp. 5-6.

NON-RESIDENCE: The absence (usually by licence) of the holder of a benefice, from that benefice.

ORDINARIES: Those who exercised jurisdiction in ecclesiastical cases, e.g. the bishops and their deputies.

PLURALISM: The term applied to the holding by a cleric of more than one benefice (or other ecclesiastical preferment) at the same time (hence 'pluralist').

Praemunire and Provisors: Various Statutes of *Praemunire*, and Statutes of Provisors, were passed during the latter half of the fourteenth century. The intention of the former was to prevent papal interference with the jurisdictional rights of the Crown in regard to presentation to benefices. The

Provisors Statutes checked papal 'provision' (or nomination) to English benefices in derogation of the rights of English patrons. ('Provisors' were the holders of such 'provisions'.) In practice the Statutes had been rarely applied, but in Henry VIII's reign the legislation was widely used and widely interpreted, especially that of *Praemunire*. The word *Praemunire* can apply to the Statute, or to the offence against the Statute, or to the writ (*Praemunire facias*) issued under the terms of the Statute.

PURGATORY: The state of suffering in which souls insufficiently purified at death wait for final expiation of sin before securing reconciliation with God. The period of time in purgatory could be shortened, and its penalties mitigated, by the saying of masses for the dead (as in chantries), and by other good works performed by the living on behalf of the dead. An acceptance of the solifidian doctrine, with its corollary – predestination to either eternal bliss or eternal condemnation – necessarily entailed rejection of the doctrine of purgatory.

SOLIFIDIAN (ISM): See JUSTIFICATION BY FAITH ALONE.

TITHES: The payment by parishioners of one tenth part of their income, usually in the form of produce and stock, to the clergy. When benefices were appropriated or impropriated (see above), the corporate body or person to whom they were assigned became the 'rector', and received the greater tithe (on crops), whilst the vicar who performed the parochial duties received the lesser tithe (chickens, eggs, etc.).

TRANSUBSTANTIATION: The eucharistic doctrine that the whole substance of the bread and wine is transformed at consecration into the whole substance of the body and blood of Christ, only the 'accidents' (i.e. the outward appearance of the bread and wine) remaining. Belief in transubstantiation had been defined as *de fide* at the Lateran Council of 1215.

SHORT LIST OF BOOKS FOR FURTHER READING

Bindoff, S. T., *Tudor England* (1950)
Brooks, P., *Thomas Cranmer's Doctrine of the Eucharist* (1965)
Dickens, A. G., *The English Reformation* (1964)
Dugmore, C. W., *The Mass and the English Reformers* (1958)
Elton, G. R., *England under the Tudors* (1955)
Heath, Peter, *The English Parish Clergy on the Eve of the Reformation* (1969)
Hughes, P., *The Reformation in England* (3 vols., 1950–4)
Hurstfield, J. (ed.), *The Reformation Crisis* (1965)
Jones, Whitney R. D., *The Tudor Commonwealth 1529–1559* (1970)
Jordan, W. K., *Edward VI: The Young King* (1968)
Jordan, W. K., *Edward VI: The Threshold of Power* (1970)
Knowles, D., *The Religious Orders in England*, vol. iii (1959)
Lehmberg, S. E., *The Reformation Parliament 1529–1536* (1970)
Loades, D. M., *The Oxford Martyrs* (1970)
Mozley, J. F., *John Foxe and his Book* (1940)
Mozley, J. F., *Coverdale and his Bibles* (1953)
Parker, T. M., *The English Reformation to 1558* (1950)
Pollard, A. F., *Wolsey* (1929)
Prescott, H. F. M., *Mary Tudor* (1953)
Ridley, J., *Thomas Cranmer* (1962)
Rupp, E. G., *Studies in the Making of the English Protestant Tradition* (1947)
Scarisbrick, J. J., *Henry VIII* (1968)
Simon, Joan, *Education and Society in Tudor England* (1966)
Williams, C. H. (ed.), *English Historical Documents, 1485–1558* (1967)
Woodward, G. W. O., *Dissolution of the Monasteries* (1966)